# CEO VISION

INSIDE

ceovision.co.uk
Jan-Feb - 2025
GLOBAL EDITION

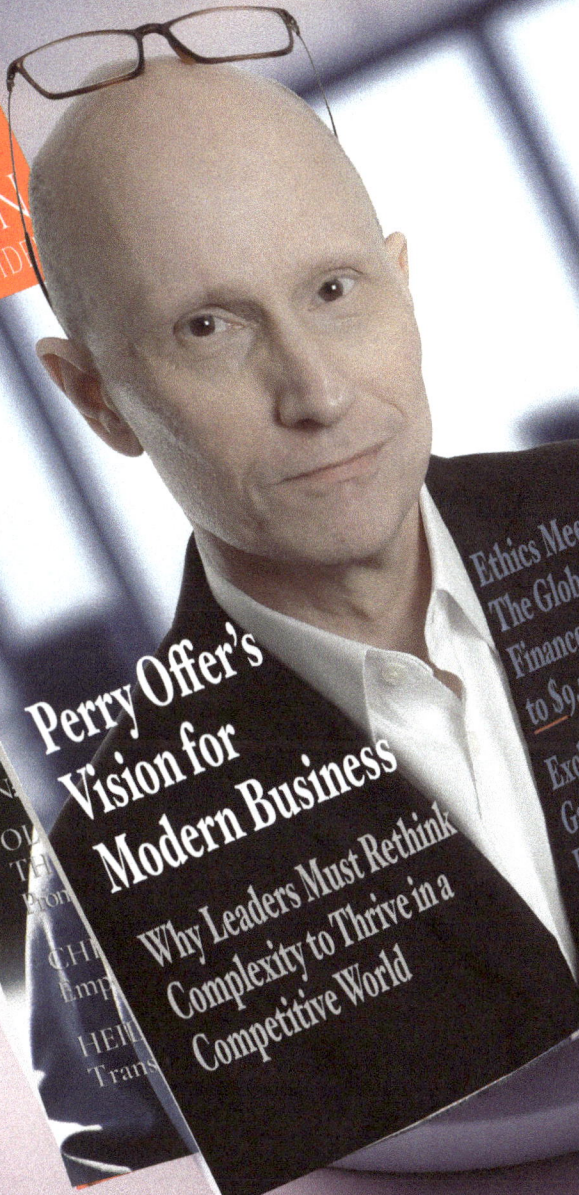

## Perry Offer's Vision for Modern Business

### Why Leaders Must Rethink Complexity to Thrive in a Competitive World

Ethics Meets Innovation: The Global Rise of Islamic Finance - projected growth to $9.7 trillion by 2029

Exclusive Interviews with Game-Changers from Tech, Finance, Retail, and More

# Dive
## Into a
## Great
## Journey

Ready to
share
your
story?

https://entrepreneurprime.co.uk
editor@entrepreneurprime.co.uk

**entrepreneur prime**
Empowers Globally

*Builds global branding, reaching over 190 countries and thousands of platforms*

A good book will keep you fascinated for days. A good bookshop for your whole life.

**Waterstones**

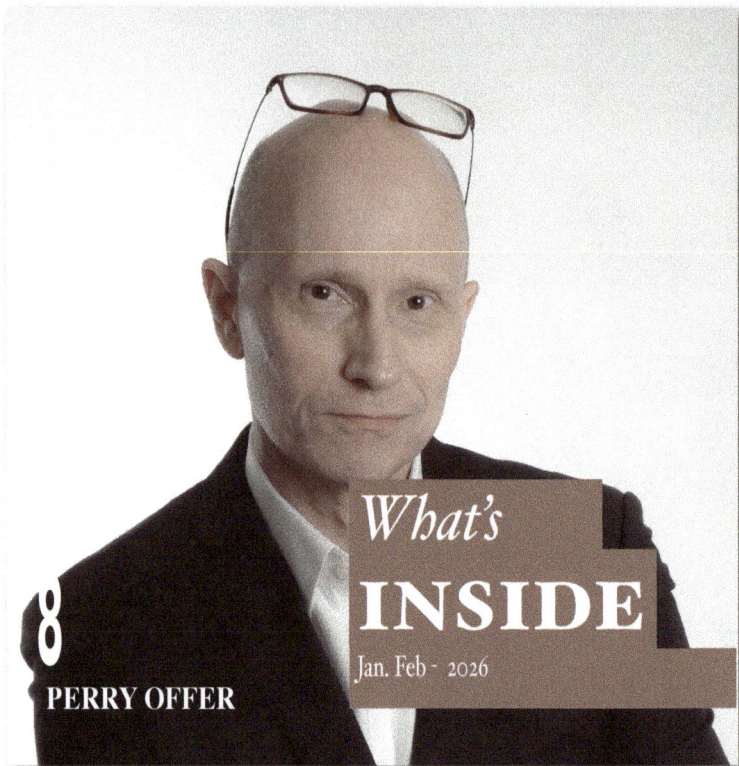

## *What's* INSIDE

Jan. Feb - 2026

**8**
**PERRY OFFER**

### *Cover*

*Perry Offer Empowering Businesses Through Innovative Strategies at Wood Hosiery*

*Driving Growth With A Focus On Simplicity and Efficiency*

*Perry Offer's entrepreneurial journey showcases the profound impact of simplifying processes, fostering resilience, and embracing change to transform companies. His principles inspire leaders to streamline operations, reject over-complication, and focus on core missions to drive sustainable success.*

**12**
**YOUSEF ALAWI**

*The global Islamic finance industry's projected growth to $9.7 trillion by 2029*

**54**

**HAN YANG**

*Discover how Han Yang blends ancient philosophies with modern technology to redefine femininity and identity*

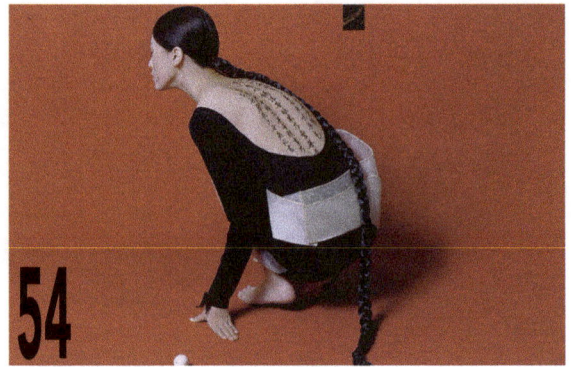

**20 & 23**
**EXECUTIVE READS**
INSIGHTS FOR EXECUTIVES

PUBLISHER: CEO VISION INSIDER, A Subsidiary of NewYox Media Group. Northway House 257 Upper St, N1 1FU, London, United Kingdom editor@entrepreneurprime.co.uk II http:entrepreneurprime.co.uk EDITORIAL: Ben F. Oncu, Editor-in-Chief, AJ Somer, Managing Editor, A. Baldie, Content Editor, Zosia Roberts, Art Editor, CONTRIBUTING EDITORS: Bernard Bale, Claudine D. Reyes, Adrian T. – We assume no responsibility for unsolicited manuscripts or art materials provided from our contributors. All content in this magazine is © copyrighted to NewYox Media. Unauthorized reproduction, distribution, or transmission of any part of this publication without written permission from the NewYox Media is strictly prohibited.

eMag

# Editor's Letter

Dear Readers,

Welcome to this edition of CEO Vision Insider, where perspectives collide to illuminate the path forward for leaders, innovators, and visionaries alike. As we reflect on the ever-shifting terrain of global commerce and economic systems, this issue encapsulates the dynamism, resilience, and ingenuity essential to navigating complexities while inspiring transformative change.

Few leaders embody the essence of clarity through adversity quite like Perry Offer. A maverick of business transformation, Perry's journey—rooted in resilience and defined by his commitment to the principle of simplicity—offers profound lessons for any leader striving to cut through the noise and achieve excellence. From revolutionising operations at Wood Hosiery to advocating for the power of simplicity in dismantling bureaucratic stagnation, Perry's philosophy reminds us that clarity of purpose and decisive action are not just strategies but mindsets essential for enduring success. In an age when businesses face unprecedented distractions, his creed of "simplification as a revolutionary act" serves as both a call to arms and a beacon of hope.

Complementing this vision, we delve into the groundbreaking work of H.E. Mr. Yousef Khalawi at the forefront of Islamic finance and ethical global investments. As the Secretary-General of the Islamic Chamber of Commerce, Industry and Agriculture, Mr. Khalawi is unleashing the full potential of values-based economic systems to drive sustainable growth. Through his leadership, the Islamic finance industry is evolving from a niche sector to a global movement aligned with ESG principles, redefining inclusivity while building ethical bridges between communities and countries. By championing education, technological innovation, and collaboration, Mr. Khalawi reminds us that ethical leadership is not an idealistic dream but a practical imperative for building equitable solutions to the world's pressing challenges.

Together, Perry Offer and Mr. Khalawi reveal the diverse paths to transformational leadership in business and finance, but their shared message transcends sectors: true visionaries build systems not just to grow but to endure. In Perry Offer's advocacy for simplicity and Mr. Khalawi's emphasis on ethics and inclusivity, we find two frameworks for navigating a world that often feels inundated with complexity—a world yearning for clarity and conscience.

As we close yet another year and prepare to welcome the opportunities of 2026, we invite you to explore the features within these pages and reflect on the themes that define our interconnected business ecosystem. Let simplicity guide your strategy, ethics steer your decision-making, and vision lead you boldly forward.

Thank you for embarking on this journey with us. Let us continue striving for purpose and impact, and as always, remember—the future belongs to those who dare to dream, simplify, and act.

Ben F. Oncu
Editor-in-Chief
CEO Vision Insider

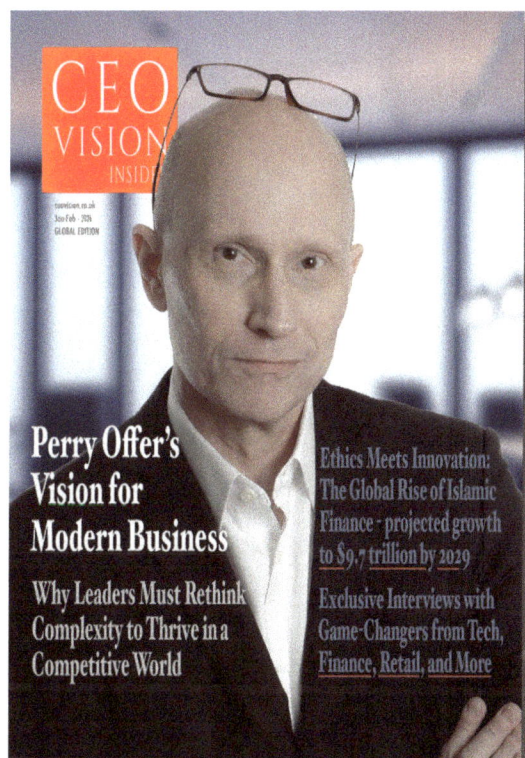

# Perry Offer Empowering Businesses Through Innovative Strategies at Wood Hosiery

## Driving Growth With A Focus On Simplicity and Efficiency

*Perry Offer's entrepreneurial journey showcases the profound impact of simplifying processes, fostering resilience, and embracing change to transform companies. His principles inspire leaders to streamline operations, reject over-complication, and focus on core missions to drive sustainable success.*

By Bernard Bale | LONDON

In today's fast-paced business environment, where complexity often reigns supreme, few voices cut through the noise with the clarity and purpose of Perry Offer. A true business maverick, Offer has distinguished himself not only by his impressive track record in transforming companies but also by his unwavering belief in the power of simplicity. His journey from a childhood marked by adversity to becoming a sought-after consultant and thought leader offers invaluable insights for entrepreneurs and established business leaders alike.

Perry's formative years were defined by a pivotal moment when, at just six years old, he faced the abrupt departure of his father. This early experience instilled in him a sense of resilience and independence that has profoundly influenced his approach to leadership and problem-solving. "At that young age, I didn't think much about my family; I just felt the need to take care of myself," he reflects. This sense of responsibility became the bedrock of his approach to business: facing challenges head-on and embracing the changes necessary for growth. "You can't

bury your head in the sand when difficulties arise. You need to confront them, prepare for change, and move forward," he emphasises.

Throughout his career, Perry has championed the idea that simplicity is the key to unlocking success. His tenure at Wood Hosiery exemplifies this philosophy. At the young age of 22, Perry took on the role of Director of Finance at a company that was performing well yet beginning to stagnate. "Stagnation can quickly lead to decline, so we knew we had to act," he recalls. Through thorough research and analysis, Perry identified an opportunity to streamline operations significantly. The company was primarily known for crafting tights to order, which often meant lengthy delivery times. By rethinking the production process—specifically, by holding a large quantity of white tights that could be dyed to order—Perry revolutionised the operation. This approach reduced delivery times from several weeks to just a few days, propelling Wood Hosiery to become a leading supplier, delivering a million pairs of tights weekly.

**Continued** *on page 10*

Continued *from page 8*

*Perry Offer is a true visionary, revolutionising businesses with clarity and simplicity. His philosophy inspires leaders to confront challenges boldly and embrace efficient solutions for transformative growth.*

Perry's success at Wood Hosiery became a cornerstone of his belief that clarity and focus are vital in business. "We discovered how to improve profits and service simultaneously without sacrificing what we already had," he explains. This fundamental principle of simplifying processes and focusing on what truly matters has become a hallmark of his work with businesses across various sectors.

*Perry's transformative leadership philosophy shaped by his early-life challenges.*

*His breakthrough approach at 22 that redesigned operations at Wood Hosiery and cut delivery times drastically.*

Beyond the walls of individual companies, Perry has become a vocal critic of the broader business climate in the UK. He argues that over-complication and mismanagement have led to a decline in British business performance. "The reality is that excessive regulation and bureaucracy are hindering innovation," he asserts. This sentiment resonates deeply in an era where businesses are often bogged down by layers of compliance and red tape. Perry passionately advocates for a renewed focus on simplicity, urging business leaders and policymakers alike to unshackle themselves from the restrictions that stifle growth. "Simplify! Step back, survey your operations, and you will quickly identify the knots of complication that breed inefficiency," he advises.

In navigating the complexities of modern commerce, Offer emphasises the importance of perspective. He encourages leaders to see technology—such as artificial intelligence—not as a be-all and end-all solution but as a tool that should enhance business operations without bringing additional complexity. "When you treat technology as a member of the team rather than just a tool, you risk complicating your business," he warns. This approach is crucial in an age where the temptation to over-rely on cutting-edge technologies can lead to confusion and inefficiency.

Reflecting on his extensive experience working with businesses of all sizes, Perry notes that one of the most common mistakes is seeking incremental changes in already complicated systems. "Introducing minor adjustments to fix a complex issue is not the solution; it's merely adding more layers of pollution to an already polluted system," he explains. Instead, he advocates for a

fundamental recognition of the necessity for simplification. "To recover from a crisis, you need to streamline your approach, eliminate what doesn't work, and return to the essentials." This principle applies universally, whether tackling a small business's challenges or addressing broader organisational issues.

Perry's insights are particularly relevant in the current global landscape, characterised by rapid change and uncertainty. He urges business leaders to remain steadfastly focused on their core missions and to resist the distractions that can lead them astray. "Opportunities may seem fleeting, but don't give up on a good idea just because it's challenging," he advises. "If your concept remains valid, perhaps the methodology needs to change, and simplification should be your guiding principle."

When discussing the greatest threats facing contemporary businesses, Perry cites the financial instability of governments and the political turmoil that often follows. "The bankruptcy of governments and an unstable geopolitical landscape pose significant challenges," he warns. He believes that addressing these overarching threats requires businesses to remain adaptable and resilient, embracing simplicity as a strategy for navigating tumultuous times.

In a contentious business environment, Perry has also tackled the issue of political correctness and its impact on innovation. He firmly believes that unnecessary regulations can burden businesses, likening them to runners encumbered by excess baggage. "The question is, who will ultimately win the race: the runner weighed down by complexity, or the one who is streamlined and focused?" he muses. Perry emphasises that many businesses have become entangled in systems and regulations that, while well-intentioned, have obscured their original vision and purpose.

Continued *on page 11*

*Perry Offer, simplifying chaos and inspiring innovation, reshaping industries one streamlined strategy at a time.*

**Continued** *from page 10*

*"AI is a tool—think of it as anything more, and it will soon want your job or your business!"*
*– Offer*

For startups and new ventures, Perry offers three guiding principles aimed at fostering success while maintaining simplicity: First, choose a specific niche, ensuring that capturing just a small percentage of demand could lead to substantial returns. Second, identify the principal aspect of your product or service that will resonate most with your target customers. Finally, focus relentlessly on delivering that core value consistently, and when you reach your goals, don't hesitate to pivot to new challenges.

Perry's emphasis on simplicity not only serves as a strategic approach to business but also reflects a deeper philosophy that can provide a sense of clarity in unsettling times. Aspiring entrepreneurs and seasoned executives alike can glean valuable lessons from his journey. The marketplace of today rewards leaders who can cut through the chaos and focus on what truly matters.

As we look to the future, the message is clear: The case for simplicity in business has never been stronger. Perry Offer's insights remind us that in an era marked by distraction and uncertainty, clarity of purpose and a commitment to simplifying operations can illuminate a path to sustained success.

Ultimately, it is those who dare to simplify in a world of complexity who will emerge as leaders, guiding their businesses to new heights in the ever-evolving landscape of global commerce.

In Perry Offer's world, simplicity is not merely a strategy; it is a philosophy that can transform organisations and reshape industries. By embracing this mindset, business leaders can not only survive the challenges of today but thrive in the opportunities of tomorrow. As Offer powerfully encapsulates, "In times of chaos, having the courage to simplify can be the most revolutionary act of all."

# Yousef Khalawi Inspires Global Transformation Through Leadership of AlBaraka Forum for Islamic Economy

## The global Islamic finance industry's projected growth to $9.7 trillion by 2029

*Yousef Khalawi leverages his expertise to expand Islamic finance globally, promoting ethics, inclusivity, and sustainability through innovation, education, and international collaboration as the Secretary-General of AlBaraka Forum.*

by Editor's Desk | **LONDON**

In a rapidly evolving financial landscape, Islamic finance is emerging as a cornerstone of ethical, sustainable, and inclusive economic systems. Driving this transformative growth is H.E. Mr. Yousef Khalawi, a globally respected leader in Islamic finance, international investments, and economic reform. With an extensive career built on solid foundations in comparative fiqh and international law, Mr. Khalawi is not only a proponent of Sharia-compliant finance but also an archetype of global ethical leadership.

As the Secretary-General of the AlBaraka Forum for Islamic Economy and the Islamic Chamber of Commerce, Industry and Agriculture, Mr. Khalawi oversees initiatives that extend economic development beyond borders and faiths, creating an inclusive financial ecosystem. Under his guidance, Islamic finance has grown into a formidable force catering to societies across both Muslim-majority and non-Muslim countries, aligning with ESG principles and driving sustainability.

A visionary leader, Yousef Khalawi has revolutionised global Islamic finance, championing ethics, sustainability, and inclusive economic growth worldwide.

### The Growth Trajectory of Islamic Finance

Islamic finance is on an impressive growth path, with projections estimating its global market size to reach $9.7 trillion by 2029. According to Mr. Khalawi, the foundation of this growth rests on the global demand for ethical and transparent financial solutions. Islamic finance—rooted in elements such as risk-sharing and avoidance of interest—naturally complements shifting investor priorities, particularly in sectors aligned with ESG standards. Its asset-backing and fair governance are increasingly appealing to ethical investors globally, further bridging the gap between traditional financial models and modern sustainability goals.

Notably, advancements in Islamic fintech are accelerating accessibility and growth. With global digital transactions expected to surpass $306 billion by 2027, digital platforms are creating bridges for underserved and emerging markets to access Sharia-compliant financial services. As Mr.

**Continued** *on page 14*

**Continued** *from page 12*

*One of the remarkable aspects of Islamic finance's growing influence is its successful entry into non-Muslim-majority markets. The United Kingdom serves as a prime example, creating regulatory clarity and tax neutrality to accommodate Sharia-compliant financial products.*

Khalawi highlights, initiatives such as cross-border sukuk issuances and robust collaborations among institutions are further helping to position Islamic finance as an indispensable part of global financial ecosystems.

> *"The strongest driver of Islamic finance is the rising global demand for ethical, transparent, and sustainability-aligned financial models."*

> *"Islamic finance is not exclusive to Muslims—it is a values-based system embracing transparency, fairness, and inclusivity for all communities."*

### A Model of Inclusivity: Non-Muslim Markets and Islamic Finance

One of the remarkable aspects of Islamic finance's growing influence is its successful entry into non-Muslim-majority markets. The United Kingdom serves as a prime example, creating regulatory clarity and tax neutrality to accommodate Sharia-compliant financial products. Mr. Khalawi underscores the importance of this inclusivity, noting that Islamic finance is not a faith-specific system—it is an ethical and values-driven system that resonates with universal principles.

To replicate such success in other non-Muslim markets, countries must focus on fostering regulatory frameworks, innovative fintech solutions, and Sharia-compliant liquidity tools. Countries like Canada, Australia, and Brazil are also exploring Islamic finance to meet rising demand for ethically aligned investment alternatives, from mortgages to pension products.

### Overcoming Barriers to Adoption

Despite promising growth, Islamic finance remains hindered by key challenges. These include misconceptions that Islamic finance is exclusive to Muslim communities, a lack of regulatory familiarity, and competition from conventional financial institutions. Mr. Khalawi identifies regulatory harmonisation, capacity-building, and public awareness campaigns as critical steps for overcoming these barriers. Countries like Kenya and Ethiopia, with limited Islamic finance expertise, have nevertheless shown that such systems can flourish under strategic leadership and educational efforts.

### Education as a Key Driver

Education is central to transforming the global perception and adoption of Islamic finance. Through initiatives at the AlBaraka Forum for Islamic Economy, Mr. Khalawi fosters academic excellence in Islamic finance. Programmes such as the Durham Islamic Finance Summer School and grants for doctoral students create opportunities for young scholars to dive deep into the field. By supporting curriculum development and simplifying concepts through digital platforms, education and public awareness are emerging as significant enablers in the modernisation of Islamic financial systems.

### Ethical Finance Meets Technological Innovation

Islamic fintech stands at the intersection of ethics and modernisation, and it is reshaping how younger generations interact with financial products. Mr. Khalawi points to the United Kingdom's burgeoning Islamic fintech scene, which features innovative platforms like robo-advisors, ethical micro-investment tools, and AI-driven automation for zakat and waqf payments. These digital solutions appeal to millennials and Gen Z entrepreneurs, offering opportunities for financial inclusion while reinforcing the ethical underpinnings of Islamic finance.

### Global Collaboration as a Catalyst

Collaboration plays a vital role in the scalability and resilience of Islamic finance. The annual AlBaraka Summit, spearheaded by Mr. Khalawi, brings together industry leaders, policymakers, and scholars from over 30 countries to foster harmonised governance, cross-border investment opportunities, and joint infrastructure projects. By creating bridges between emerging markets and established financial hubs like London and Kuala Lumpur, these collaborations strengthen the global Islamic financial ecosystem.

### A Vision for the Future

Mr. Khalawi envisions Islamic finance as a key contributor to ethical capitalism and inclusive global growth. Its emphasis on asset-backed structures uniquely positions it to drive developments in housing, renewa-

**Continued** *on page 15*

*Yousef Khalawi, Secretary-General of AlBaraka Forum, revolutionises Islamic finance by combining ethical principles with sustainable, global financial innovation.*

*Notably, advancements in Islamic fintech are accelerating accessibility and growth. With global digital transactions expected to surpass $306 billion by 2027, digital platforms are creating bridges for underserved and emerging markets to access Sharia-compliant financial services.*

**Continued** *from page 14*

ble energy, and socially impactful sectors. Moreover, tools like profit-and-loss sharing, interest-free financing, and community-driven initiatives such as zakat and waqf provide a blueprint for an equitable financial system.

Under Mr. Khalawi's leadership, Islamic finance is transitioning from a niche to a global movement, showcasing that economic success can thrive within a framework of ethics, transparency, and sustainability. His pioneering work continues to bridge cultural divides, redefine financial inclusivity, and inspire global markets to adopt a values-based approach to finance.

As the world grapples with challenges of inequality and environmental crises, Islamic finance stands out as a beacon of hope—one that proves we can build systems benefiting all segments of society. Thanks to leaders like H.E. Mr. Yousef Khalawi, the journey toward a sustainable and inclusive global economy is not only possible but already well underway.

# Dr. Terence McIvor, Innovator Behind SynapGen®, Revolutionizes Coaching and Education with Groundbreaking Transformational Systems

## Harnessing Science, Psychology, And Innovation

## To Unlock True Human Potential

*Dr. Terence McIvor's SynapGen® Transformational Coaching System bridges neuroscience, NLP, and hypnotherapy to foster growth, resilience, creativity, and mental wellness, redefining coaching and education for individuals and businesses alike.*

by CEO Vision Inside Staff

Embarking on a journey through the synapses of innovation and transformation, New Yox Media delves into the extraordinary endeavours of Dr. Terence McIvor, widely revered as the Synaptic Trainer®. A paragon of interdisciplinary mastery, Dr. McIvor's remarkable integration of chemistry, hypnotherapy, and neuro-linguistic programming has crafted a new paradigm of entrepreneurial and educational excellence. His philosophy, while straightforward, is profoundly impactful: harness the

*Dr. McIvor's visionary leadership and interdisciplinary expertise transform lives, blending science with personal growth to create lasting impact worldwide.*

mind's power to create change, both in education and in the broader scope of personal and professional development.

As a trailblazer in the science of transformation, Dr. McIvor has revolutionized personal growth and professional development methodologies. Founder of the **International Guild of Hypnotherapy, NLP, and 3 Principles Practitioners and Trainers (IGH3P)**, he has elevated the standards in these fields with unparalleled dedication. More than that, his **Sales Doctor Counselling and Life Coaching Clinic** serves as a bridge between business strategies and psychological insights, empowering individuals to cultivate success with mental well-being.

From his roots in the historic city of Derry, Northern Ireland, Dr. McIvor's academic and professional trajectory reflects an unwavering commitment to growth and discovery. Holding a biochemistry degree, a PhD in chemical education, and a master's in psychology with expertise in neuroscience, he exemplifies the fusion of knowledge, passion, and purpose. His influence as a recognized authority in STEM and science education, certified by OFQUAL in the U.K., coupled with his global contributions as a visiting professor and esteemed panellist, has indelibly reshaped learning landscapes.

However, Dr. McIvor's most compelling contributions center on alleviating human suffering. His pioneering neuroplastic pain reprocessing techniques reflect his commitment to helping individuals overcome chronic pain, proving that the mind possesses the ability to transcend physical limitations. His revolutionary **SynapGen Transformational Coaching System®** epitomizes his life's work—integrating science, psychology, and innovation into a holistic approach to unlock human potential. In this exclusive feature, we explore the inspirations, methods, and vision of Dr. Terence McIvor as he reshapes coaching, education, and personal growth on an extraordinary scale.

### The Birth of SynapGen®

Dr. McIvor's inspiration for the **SynapGen Transformational Coaching System®** stemmed from an innate desire to leverage the brain's dynamic capabilities to drive personal and professional growth. Fascinated by the concept of brain plasticity—the brain's ability to adapt and rewire through experience—he envisioned a coaching system that could profoundly enhance cognitive and emotional well-being. "The dynamic nature of neuroscience suggests possibilities to fundamentally shift thought patterns, behaviors, and emotions," he explains. By bridging advanced neuroscience with psychological method-ologies, Dr. McIvor created a transformative coaching framework that enables individuals to unlock their deepest potential for success.

### Personalization at Its Core

What sets the SynapGen® system apart is its emphasis on customized, sustainable development. Dr. McIvor designed SynapGen® as a comprehensive spectrum of targeted programs, each aimed at addressing specific growth areas for participants. By tailoring learning experiences to align with the unique objectives of each individual, SynapGen® champions a truly personalized approach to development.

Programs under the SynapGen® banner include **NociPath** for addressing chronic pain, **Creative Edge** for sparking innovation, and **Communication Advantage,** which fosters interpersonal and leadership communication skills. Participants embark on guided, individualized journeys that empower them to achieve significant breakthroughs in both their personal and professional lives.

### Combating Chronic Pain with Noci-Path™

Of particular distinction within SynapGen® is the **Noc-**

**Continued** *on page 18*

# SynapGen®
## Transformational Coaching

*Dr. Terence McIvor, The Synaptic Trainer®, Unlocking Transformation Through Science, Innovation, And Empowerment*

DR. TERENCE MCIVOR

Founder of the International Guild of Hypnotherapy,
NLP and 3 Principles Practitioners and Trainers
(IGH3P®)

**Continued** *from page 16*

**iPath Training and Coaching System™**, a program designed to address chronic pain through an integrated approach. Dr.

*Dr. McIvor is an exceptional visionary, seamlessly merging neuroscience and psychology to pioneer SynapGen®. His dedication to empowering individuals, fostering resilience, and igniting transformation sets a new standard in personal development.*

McIvor explains the multifaceted methodologies employed, which combine hypnotherapy, neuro-linguistic programming (NLP), neuroscience coaching, somatic tracking, and vagal nerve therapy. This innovative model tackles chronic pain not only at the physical level but also at its psychological root, helping patients build resilience and retrain their responses to pain.

"Hypnotherapy enables recipients to access the subconscious mind, modifying their perceptions of pain, while NLP works to transform their pain-related thought patterns," Dr. McIvor elaborates. In addition, coaching techniques driven by neuroscience leverage brain plasticity, empowering participants to establish new and healthier neural pathways that promote long-term management and relief.

### Enhancing Employee Wellness and Workplace Productivity

Recognizing the growing demand for employee well-being in today's high-pressure work environments, Dr. McIvor designed SynapGen® with an **Employee Wellness Programme** as a cornerstone. The program focuses on equipping employees with the skills to manage stress effectively, enhance emotional resilience, and establish healthier coping mechanisms.

"Healthier employees are more engaged, creative, and

productive," says Dr. McIvor. "Promoting mental well-being is not just an individual responsibility; it's a critical strategy for business success." By addressing workplace stress and fostering environments that prioritize mental health, businesses can experience increased productivity and employee satisfaction.

### Creative Thinking with Creative Edge™

To remain competitive in an ever-evolving world, innovation and creativity must be cultivated. That's precisely the goal of SynapGen's **Creative Edge™ program**, which inspires participants to embrace out-of-the-box thinking. Through immersive exercises like brainstorming sessions, scenario simulations, and structured creative challenges, participants are taught to break free from traditional thought patterns and embrace innovative solutions.

"These techniques encourage participants to develop a mindset of experimentation and curiosity," Dr. McIvor observes. By doing so, the Creative Edge™ program enables participants to enhance problem-solving capabilities and apply creative thinking in both their personal and professional endeavors.

### Developing Communication and Leadership Skills

Interpersonal relationships and communication skills are integral to thriving in a world driven by human connections. Dr. McIvor's **Communication Advantage™ program** equips participants with practical training techniques aimed at empathetic listening and persuasive speech. Using the principles of NLP, the program ensures participants can refine how they connect, express thoughts, and influence others.

"Effective communication is not just a skill; it's the bridge to leadership, successful persuasion, and building trust," Dr. McIvor explains. Whether the goal is to excel in collaborative environments, close vital business deals, or foster personal connections, Communication Advantage™ offers a multifaceted toolkit for success.

### The Mind-Body Connection: Rejuvenise 360™

A key element of long-term well-being, Dr. McIvor emphasizes, is the integration of physical fitness and nutrition with cognitive and emotional wellness. The **Rejuvenise 360™ program** addresses this by leveraging brain-boosting diets, such as the Mediterranean and MIND diets, as well as tailored fitness programs to enhance not only physical health but also cognitive function and emotional stability.

"Exercise and nutrition play pivotal roles in neurogenesis and neuroplasticity," explains Dr. McIvor. By incorporating these elements into the coaching framework, SynapGen® takes a holistic approach to empowerment, enabling participants to develop sharper focus, improved mood, and greater overall health.

### Building Resilience for the Long Game

Building lasting resilience is integral to achieving growth and self-fulfillment, and Dr. McIvor has designed SynapGen® with this philosophy in mind. The system ensures participants don't just make temporary changes but are equipped to sustain these transformations over time. Exercises promoting emotional regulation, cognitive flexibility, and stress management serve as the foundation for fostering resilient mental frameworks.

Participants leave the program with a toolkit of skills that empowers them to navigate future challenges and uncertainties with confidence. "True growth stems from resilience," says Dr. McIvor, "which is why our methods focus on instilling habits and skills that last well beyond the completion of the program."

### Preparing the Next Generation of Coaches

The SynapGen® qualifications offer an extensive learning path for individuals aspiring to serve as transformative coaches. Starting at the foundational level with the **SynapGen® Certified Practitioner**, coaches gain the fundamental tools of neurosci-

*The Creative Edge™ program is designed to foster innovative thinking through various exercises that challenge the conventional thought processes.*

**(IGH3P®)**

ence and coaching methodology. Progressing to advanced levels, they focus on specialized areas, including emotional intelligence and pain management. Finally, the **SynapGen® Master Trainer** certification equips coaches with skills to lead large-scale initiatives and mentor other coaches.

"The structure is designed to provide progressive levels of learning," explains Dr. McIvor. "Our certifications ensure that coaches are fully equipped to guide transformative journeys for individuals and organizations alike."

### Fostering Community and Collaboration

Integral to the SynapGen® program is the emphasis on community support, which extends beyond structured coursework. Dr. McIvor has incorporated virtual meetups, forums, and webinars to create an active community of like-minded individuals dedicated to personal growth and professional collaboration.

"Community is the lifeblood of continuous development," he says. "Our goal is to ensure that every SynapGen participant remains connected to an evolving network of support, inspiration, and shared success."

Source: Entrepreneur Prime.

# THE ETHICS OF COACHING

## ABOUT DR. MCIVOR
### Founder of the International Guild of Hypnotherapy, NLP and 3 Principles Practitioners and Trainers

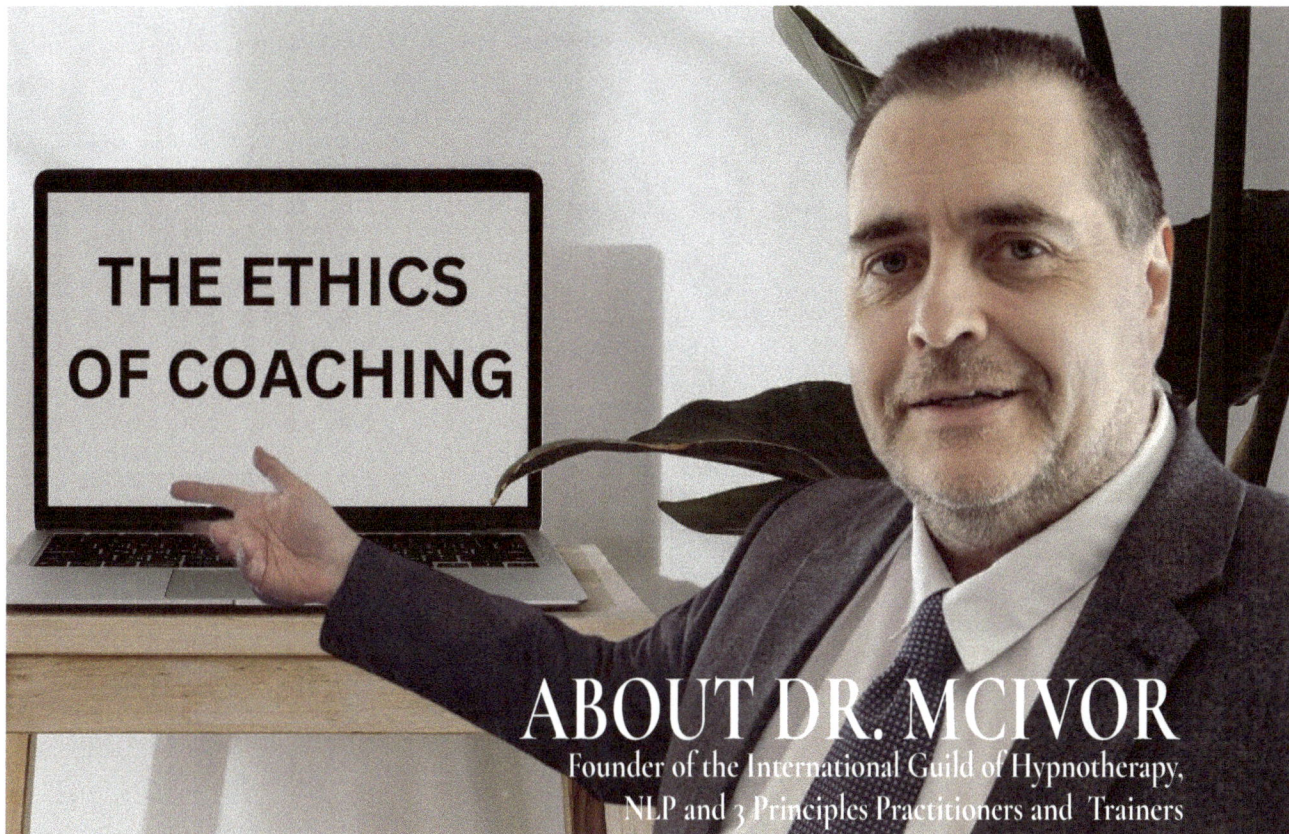

D r. Terence McIvor, also known as the Synaptic Trainer®, is an esteemed Irish entrepreneur, academic, chemistry professor, transformative coach, clinical hypnotherapist, and expert trainer in neuro-linguistic programming (NLP) and hypnotherapy. His extensive career covers a range of disciplines, including education, therapeutic practices, and personal development, highlighting his dedication to enhancing learning and transformational processes using a blend of science and psychology. Dr. McIvor's work has been pivotal in improving access to quality education and personal development across the globe.

## Professional Foundations and Contributions

Dr. McIvor founded the International Guild of Hypnotherapy, NLP, and 3 Principles Practitioners and Trainers (IGH3P), setting high standards in these fields. He also established the Sales Doctor Counselling and Life Coaching Clinic, renowned for its innovative integration of neuro-sensory psychology, hypnotherapy, and chronic pain reprocessing, specifically tailored for entrepreneurs and business professionals.

Renowned for his contributions to leadership training, sales performance, neurolinguistic psychology, and critical problem-solving, Dr. McIvor employs advanced neuroplastic pain reprocessing techniques as a pain reprocessing coach, helping those afflicted with chronic pain.

## Early Life and Education

Dr. McIvor was born and raised in Derry, Nort- hern Ireland, where he completed his early education at St. Joseph's School. He then earned a national diploma in science from the Northwest Institute of Further and Higher Education and obtained a biochemistry degree from Ulster University. He furthered his academic pursuits at the same university, obtaining postgraduate certificates in Further and Higher Education and Educational Technology.

Dr. McIvor earned a PhD in chemical education from Bundelkhand University in 2012 and a master's degree in computer applications in 2014. He also holds a master's in psychology, focusing on neuroscience and psychiatric applications, from Manipur International University, where he was appointed chair of psychology and neuroscience therapy.

## Career Achievements and Milestones

Dr. McIvor began his professional journey as a textile chemist at Lintrend and later joined Seagate Technology as an assistant engineer in 1999. His career in education spans over two decades, during which he has developed and led numerous academic initiatives. Notably, the Office of Qualifications and Examinations Regulation (OFQUAL) in the U.K. has recognised him as a STEM and science expert.

His academic career took off at the North West Further and Higher Education Institute in Ireland, where he became head of vocational education and quality assurance within the Science and Mathematics Section. His efforts there included creating an innovative Applied Mathematics Support Centre, which helped students overcome challenges in mathematics.

## Global Influence and Contributions

Dr. McIvor has also made significant contributions to global educational and humanitarian projects. He served as a Visiting Professor of Bio-Physical Chemistry at Afriford University in Benin and a visiting scholar at Bundelkhand University, Jhansi. He has reviewed scientific literature as a panellist recognised for the Biomedical and Therapeutic Sciences journal in India and served as a certification specialist at the American Institute of Chemists in Philadelphia, Pennsylvania.

In 2017, Dr. McIvor founded the Academy for International Science and Research (AISR) in the UK, where he engages in teaching, coaching, training, and research. He has been actively involved in various professional bodies, providing certified training in medical and dental hypnosis, and his academy has received recognition from the Hypnotherapy Directory U.K.

## Continued Legacy and Impact

Dr. McIvor is also a coach mentor for EMCC UK and the IRCM.CIC, holding a fellow-level membership with the Association for Coaching. His expertise and authority in neuroscience, hypnotherapy, NLP, pain reprocessing, and coaching have been recognised globally, with accolades such as the BRAINZ 500 Global Award and featured in prestigious publications.

Through his extensive career, Dr. Terry McIvor has continued to be a leading figure in science,

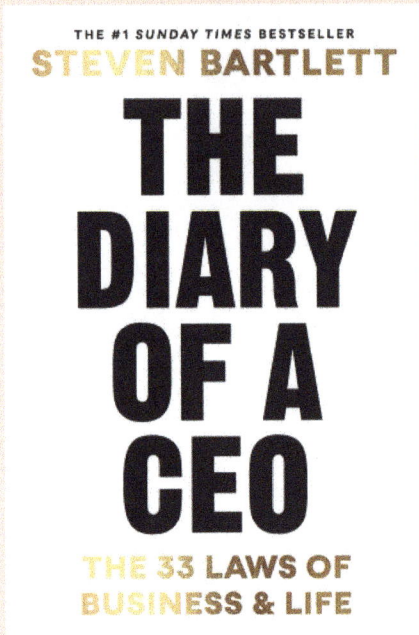

## THE DIARY OF A CEO
### by Steven Bartlett

*"Bartlett's book is a beacon of wisdom, guiding readers to embrace authenticity and resilience on their journey to greatness."*

Steven Bartlett's *The Diary of a CEO* is a refreshing departure from conventional business literature, offering a profound exploration of timeless principles that transcend industry boundaries. With a compelling mix of personal anecdotes, global insights, and psychological research, Bartlett presents a roadmap for achieving greatness in both business and life.

Unlike typical business strategy books, Bartlett delves into the fundamental laws that underpin success, emphasizing the importance of self-awareness, resilience, and continuous learning. Drawing from his own entrepreneurial journey and interviews with thousands of successful individuals, Bartlett distills invaluable wisdom that resonates with readers at every stage of their professional and personal development.

Through engaging storytelling and practical advice, Bartlett challenges readers to redefine success and embrace a mindset of growth and authenticity. Whether you're an aspiring entrepreneur or a seasoned leader, *The Diary of a CEO* offers invaluable insights that will inspire you to chart your own path to greatness.

In a world where success is often measured by external achievements, Bartlett reminds us that true fulfillment comes from within. This book is a compelling reminder that greatness is not just about what we achieve, but who we become along the way.

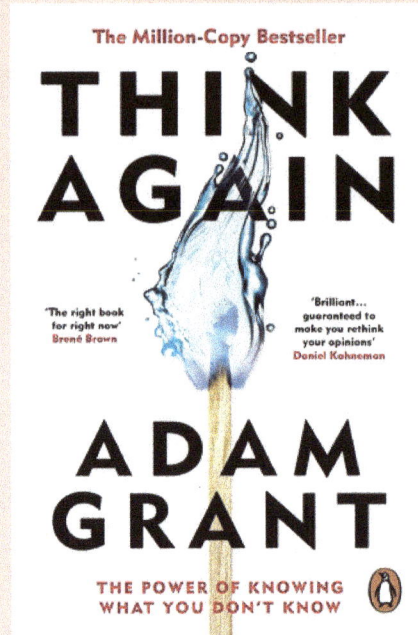

## THINK AGAIN
### by Adam Grant

*"Grant's 'Think Again' is a beacon of insight, urging us to embrace the power of flexible thinking in a changing world."*

*Think Again* by Adam Grant is a compelling exploration of the transformative power of embracing intellectual humility. In a world evolving at breakneck speed, Grant asserts that the ability to adapt and revise our beliefs is paramount. Through captivating anecdotes and rigorous research, he persuasively argues that our capacity to rethink, unlearn, and update our perspectives is a skill that transcends traditional notions of intelligence.

Drawing from insightful conversations with luminaries like Elon Musk and political strategists, Grant illuminates the necessity of challenging entrenched ideas and fostering an environment conducive to intellectual growth. He deftly navigates the terrain of cognitive biases and social pressures, offering practical strategies for cultivating a mindset open to continual learning.

*Think Again* is not merely a book; it's a manifesto for intellectual agility in an era defined by uncertainty and complexity. Grant's prose is engaging, his arguments cogent, and his message timely. This million-copy bestseller is essential reading for anyone seeking to navigate the currents of change with grace and wisdom.

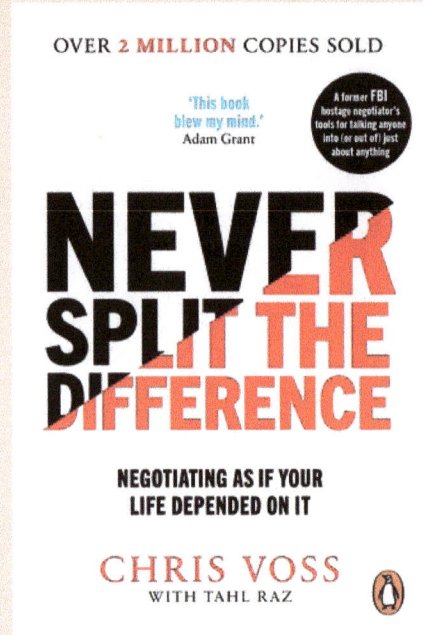

## NEVER SPLIT THE DIFFERENCE
### by Chris Voss and Tahl Raz

*Never Split the Difference is a game-changer, offering actionable strategies for negotiations in any scenario. A must-read for success-seekers.*

*Never Split the Difference* by Chris Voss and Tahl Raz is a masterclass in negotiation tactics, distilled from Voss's illustrious career as an FBI hostage negotiator. This book isn't just about bargaining for hostages' lives; it's a comprehensive guide applicable to myriad real-world situations, from business deals to personal relationships.

Voss's nine principles, outlined with clarity and supported by gripping anecdotes, offer a roadmap to navigate the most challenging conversations. The authors emphasize the importance of empathy, active listening, and understanding the emotional drivers behind every negotiation. Voss's approach goes beyond traditional win-win strategies; it's about forging genuine connections and achieving mutually beneficial outcomes.

What sets *Never Split the Difference* apart is its practicality. Each principle is accompanied by actionable techniques that readers can immediately apply. Whether it's the "mirroring" technique to build rapport or the art of crafting calibrated questions to uncover hidden information, Voss equips readers with tools to navigate complex interactions with confidence.

The book's acclaim from experts like Adam Grant and publications such as The Guardian speaks to its impact and relevance. Steven Bartlett's endorsement underscores its universal applicability, resonating with readers across diverse backgrounds and professions.

In a world where negotiation is an essential skill, "Never Split the Difference" stands out as a definitive guide. Engaging, insightful, and immensely practical, it's a must-read for anyone looking to enhance their negotiation prowess and achieve success in all facets of life.

**HOW GREAT LEADERS BUILD UNSTOPPABLE TEAMS**

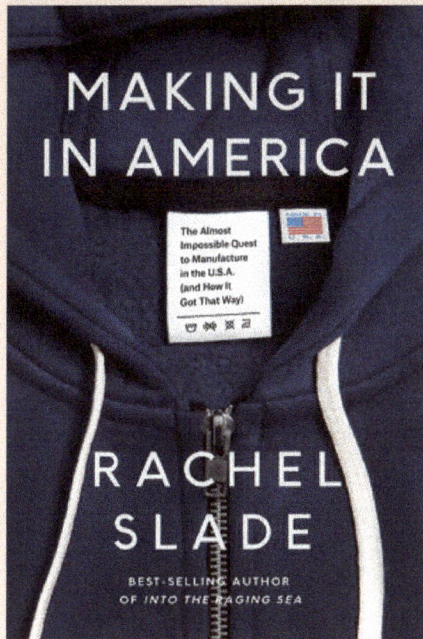

MAKING IT IN AMERICA

The Almost Impossible Quest to Manufacture in the U.S.A. (and How It Got That Way)

RACHEL SLADE

BEST-SELLING AUTHOR OF *INTO THE RAGING SEA*

**ALL IN**

MIKE MICHALOWICZ

Author of *PROFIT FIRST* and *THE PUMPKIN PLAN*

NEW YORK TIMES BESTSELLER

**RICH AF**

The Winning Money Mindset That Will Change Your Life

Vivian Tu

YOUR RICH BFF

## MAKING IT IN AMERICA
### By Rachel Slade

## NOT YOUR CHINA DOLL
### By Katie Gee Salisbury

## HOW TO BE OLD
### By Lyn Slater

*Making It in America is a compelling exploration of the complexities of American manufacturing, weaving personal narratives into a broader societal tapestry.*

*Making It in America* by Rachel Slade takes readers on a poignant journey through the complexities of American manufacturing, woven into the personal narrative of Ben and Whitney Waxman. As they endeavor to create an American-made, ethically sourced sweatshirt, their story encapsulates the challenges and aspirations of a nation grappling with its industrial identity.

Slade's narrative skillfully navigates through the landscape of labor rights, economic shifts, and global politics, offering a compelling examination of the manufacturing industry's impact on American society. From the cotton fields of Mississippi to the garment districts of New York City, the Waxmans' quest illuminates the intertwined histories of labor activism and industrial innovation.

Through their struggles with personal demons and external obstacles, Ben and Whitney emerge as emblematic figures, embodying the resilience and determination required to pursue the American dream in an ever-changing landscape. Slade deftly captures the zeitgeist of contemporary America, where questions of ethics, sustainability, and economic revitalization intersect.

*Making It in America* is not just a story about one couple's journey; it's a reflection of the broader narrative shaping the nation's future. Slade's insightful analysis and engaging prose make this book essential reading for anyone interested in the intricacies of American manufacturing and its enduring significance in the global economy.

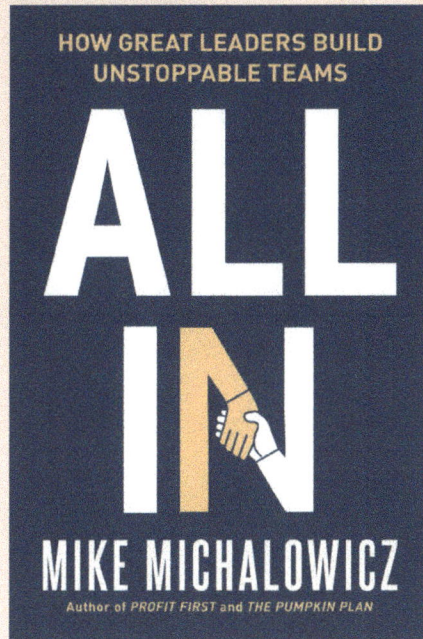

*"Rothenberg's 'Not Your China Doll' captivates with vivid storytelling, celebrating Anna May Wong's groundbreaking journey in Hollywood."*

*Not Your China Doll* by Ben Rothenberg delves into the captivating journey of Anna May Wong, the trailblazing Asian American movie star of Hollywood's golden era. Rothenberg skillfully navigates Wong's ascent from humble beginnings in Los Angeles to international stardom, shedding light on her struggles against typecasting and racial stereotypes in the film industry.

Set against the glitz and glamor of 1920s Los Angeles, Rothenberg paints a vivid portrait of Wong as a legendary beauty and fashion icon who defied societal expectations. Through meticulous research and engaging prose, he chronicles her rise to fame in Douglas Fairbanks's The Thief of Bagdad and her subsequent rebellion against Hollywood's discriminatory practices.

Wong's bold decision to challenge Hollywood's racism by seeking opportunities abroad is portrayed with poignancy and admiration. Rothenberg masterfully captures the essence of Wong's audacity and resilience as she navigates through a world of capricious directors, glamorous parties, and far-flung love affairs.

*Not Your China Doll* is a compelling tribute to a pioneering artist who paved the way for future generations of Asian American actors. Rothenberg's debut book is a must-read for anyone interested in cinema history and the ongoing struggle for representation in the entertainment industry.

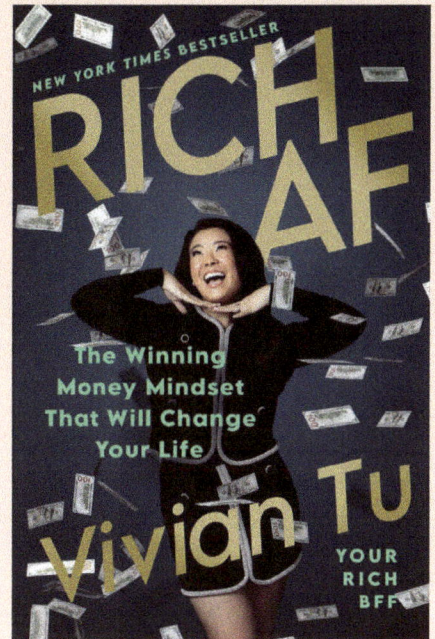

*"How to Be Old" by Lyn Slater empowers readers to embrace aging boldly, redefine beauty standards, and live life on their terms.*

*How to Be Old* by Lyn Slater, also known as the "Accidental Icon," is a refreshing and empowering memoir that challenges societal norms surrounding aging. Through her personal journey documented over a decade, Slater proves that age is merely a number and should not limit one's ability to live boldly and authentically.

Slater's candid storytelling and unapologetic embrace of her gray hair and wrinkles serve as an inspiration for readers of all ages. She rejects the notion of fading into the background as one grows older and instead encourages readers to redefine their perceptions of aging. Her message resonates deeply, emphasizing the importance of self-acceptance and embracing change with optimism and creativity.

With wit and wisdom, Slater demonstrates that the process of reinvention knows no bounds. She encourages readers to challenge societal standards of beauty and youth, advocating for a more inclusive and empowering definition of successful aging. Through her narrative, Slater showcases the potential for growth, connection, and creativity in every stage of life.

*How to Be Old* is not just a memoir; it's a manifesto for living life on one's own terms. Slater's fearless approach to aging serves as a beacon of hope and empowerment for readers seeking to navigate the complexities of getting older. This paradigm-shifting book is a must-read for anyone looking to embrace the fullness of life at any age.

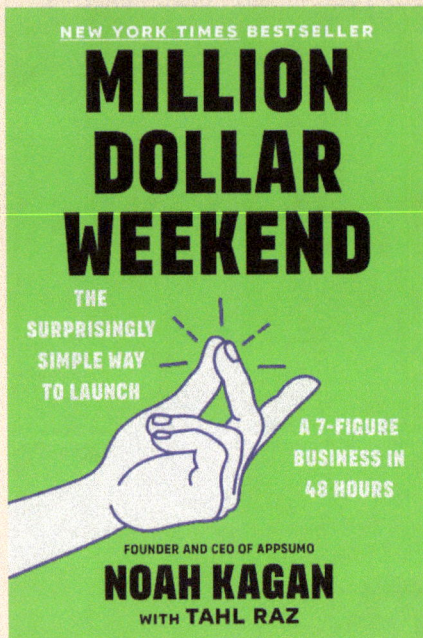

## MILLION DOLLAR WEEKEND
*by Noah Kagan*

*Million Dollar Weekend is a game-changing blueprint for aspiring entrepreneurs, offering practical steps to launch a successful business quickly.*

Million Dollar Weekend by Noah Kagan is a game-changer for aspiring entrepreneurs, offering a roadmap to launch a successful business in just one weekend. Kagan's no-nonsense approach cuts through the noise of traditional entrepreneurship advice, providing practical steps to turn ideas into profitable ventures. With his own experience of building seven-figure businesses, Kagan inspires readers to overcome fear and take action.

The book addresses common barriers to entrepreneurship, debunking myths and providing actionable solutions. Kagan emphasizes the importance of finding "Creator's Courage" to push through uncertainties and embrace the journey of building a business. His "Million Dollar Weekend" Process simplifies the daunting task of acquiring customers and automating operations, making entrepreneurship accessible to anyone willing to take the leap.

Written in Kagan's signature candid style, Million Dollar Weekend is a refreshing departure from conventional business guides. It's a must-read for anyone tired of the nine-to-five grind and ready to pursue financial freedom on their own terms. Whether you're a seasoned entrepreneur or a first-time business owner, this book offers invaluable insights to kickstart your journey to success.

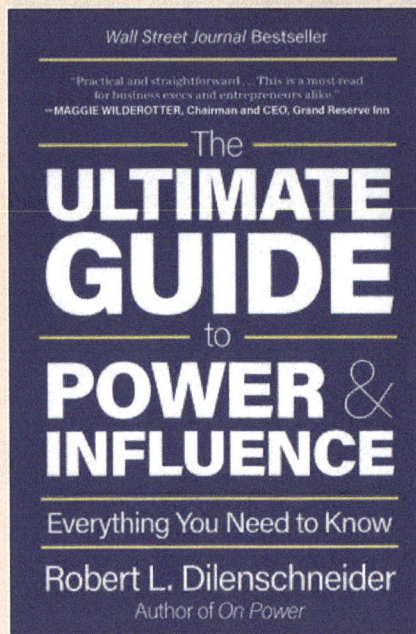

## THE ULTIMATE GUIDE TO POWER & INFLUENCE
*by Robert L. Dilenschneider*

*The Ultimate Guide to Power & Influence is a game-changer, offering indispensable wisdom for success in today's dynamic business world.*

In The Ultimate Guide to Power & Influence, Robert L. Dilenschneider offers a comprehensive roadmap for navigating the complexities of modern business. With technology and globalization reshaping the landscape, Dilenschneider emphasizes the importance of not just acquiring power, but also wielding it wisely.

Drawing on his extensive experience as a respected consultant and founder of The Dilenschneider Group, Dilenschneider provides readers with a wealth of intellectual, technical, and moral tools essential for success in today's competitive environment. From seizing opportunities in times of crisis to effectively managing networks and leveraging social media, this book offers practical insights gleaned from real-world examples and the wisdom of industry leaders.

As a Wall Street Journal, USA Today, and Publishers Weekly bestseller, "The Ultimate Guide to Power & Influence" has earned acclaim for its relevance and timeliness. Whether you're a seasoned executive or just starting out in your career, Dilenschneider's authoritative guidance equips you to navigate the ever-evolving business landscape with confidence and competence.

With its blend of strategic advice and practical wisdom, this book is an indispensable resource for anyone seeking to enhance their power and influence in the modern world. Whether you're aiming for personal success or contributing to the prosperity of society at large, Dilenschneider's insights offer valuable guidance for achieving your goals with integrity and impact.

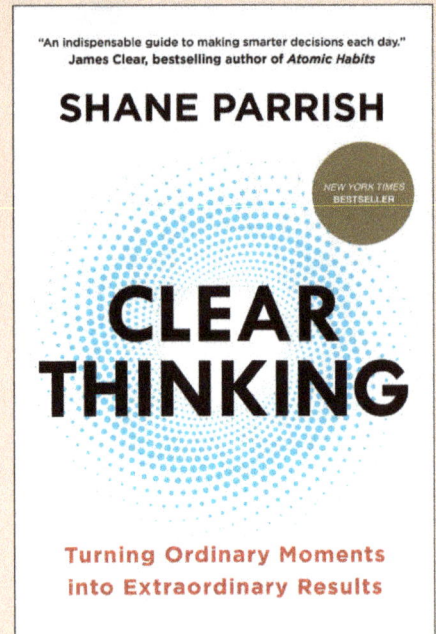

## CLEAR THINKING
*By Shane Parrish*

*Shane Parrish's 'Clear Thinking' is a transformative beacon, illuminating the path to intentional living with profound insights and practical guidance.*

Shane Parrish's Clear Thinking is a beacon illuminating the often overlooked path to success and fulfillment. With a deft hand, Parrish guides readers through the labyrinth of human cognition, revealing the hidden opportunities for clarity that lie within everyday moments.

In a world fraught with distractions and pressures, Parrish's insights couldn't be more timely. Drawing from a rich tapestry of anecdotes and research, he unveils the mechanisms of thought that shape our lives, urging us to seize control of our cognitive destiny.

Clear Thinking is more than just a book—it's a roadmap to empowerment. Parrish equips readers with the tools to recognize pivotal moments and harness the full power of their reasoning faculties. Through the lens of behavioral science, he demystifies the autopilot mode that so often dictates our actions, empowering us to chart a deliberate course toward our goals.

Accessible yet profound, Clear Thinking is a game-changer for anyone seeking to elevate their decision-making prowess. Whether you're striving for professional success or personal fulfillment, Parrish's wisdom offers invaluable guidance for navigating life's complexities with intentionality and insight.

In a crowded landscape of self-help literature, Clear Thinking stands out as a beacon of clarity—a must-read for anyone committed to mastering the art of thoughtful living.

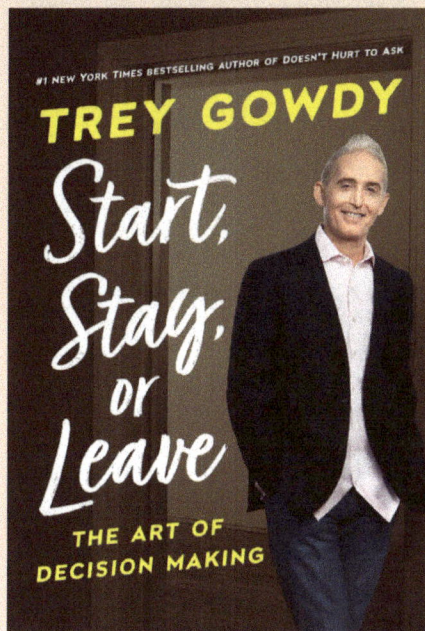

## START, STAY, OR LEAVE
### By Trey Gowdy

*Start, Stay, or Leave by Trey Gowdy is a beacon of practical wisdom, offering invaluable guidance for life's pivotal decisions.*

Start, Stay, or Leave by Trey Gowdy presents a compelling framework for decision-making that resonates with both practicality and profound insights. Gowdy's personal journey, interwoven with his unique decision-making tool, offers readers a roadmap for navigating life's pivotal moments.

Drawing from his experiences in the courtroom and political arena, Gowdy distills complex choices into three simple options: start, stay, or leave. Through anecdotes and hard-earned wisdom, he illustrates how this framework has guided his own life decisions, from career transitions to personal relationships.

What sets this book apart is its relatable tone and conversational style. Reading it feels like a candid conversation with a trusted friend, as Gowdy shares his successes, failures, and lessons learned along the way. His advice is practical yet profound, encouraging readers to craft their vision of success, consult their dreams with wisdom, and balance logic with emotion when facing challenges.

Start, Stay, or Leave is not just a guidebook; it's a companion for life's journey. Filled with humor, heartbreak, and timeless storytelling, it equips readers with the confidence to approach trajectory-changing decisions and embrace the outcomes, knowing they've made the best choice they could. Whether you're at a crossroads or seeking clarity in your path, Gowdy's insights offer invaluable guidance for navigating life's complexities with purpose and conviction.

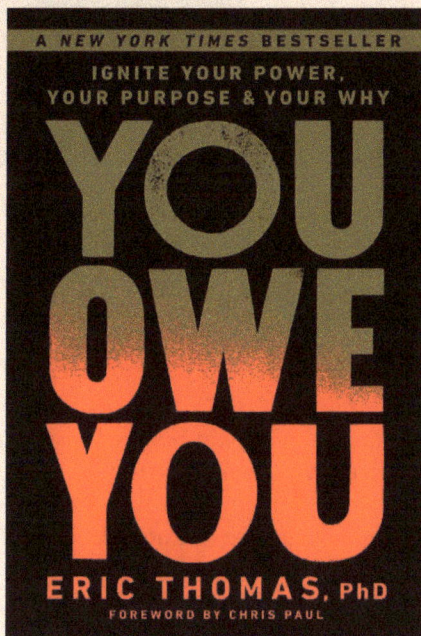

## YOU OWE YOU
### By Eric Thomas, PhD

*You Owe You is a transformative masterpiece, Eric Thomas's inspiring words ignite the spark needed for personal evolution.*

You Owe You by Eric Thomas, PhD, is not just a book; it's a life-altering experience encapsulated in pages. With a voice that resonates with urgency and authenticity, Thomas compels readers to shed the shackles of self-doubt and seize control of their destinies. Drawing from his own journey of overcoming adversity, Thomas delivers a powerful message that success is not reserved for the chosen few but is within the grasp of anyone willing to take ownership of their lives.

Through poignant anecdotes and practical advice, Thomas navigates readers through the labyrinth of self-discovery, urging them to confront their fears, identify their passions, and relentlessly pursue their dreams. His insights transcend the boundaries of age, race, and circumstance, offering a roadmap to empowerment for anyone seeking transformation.

What sets You Owe You apart is its unwavering belief in the individual's capacity for greatness. Thomas's unwavering conviction that every person possesses the potential to rewrite their story infuses the narrative with hope and possibility. Whether you're a CEO or a high school dropout, this book serves as a beacon of inspiration, guiding you towards a life of purpose and fulfillment.

In essence, You Owe You is more than a book; it's a manifesto for reclaiming one's power and embracing the boundless opportunities that await. Eric Thomas's compelling prose and profound wisdom make this a must-read for anyone ready to embark on a journey of self-discovery and personal growth.

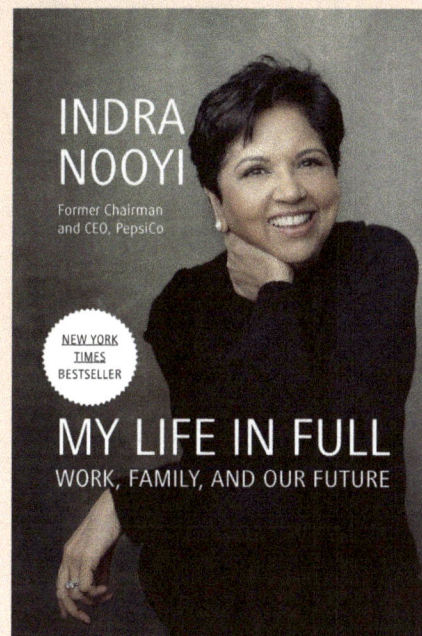

## MY LIFE IN FULL
### By Indra Nooyi

*Indra Nooyi's "My Life in Full" is an inspiring testament to leadership, resilience, and the pursuit of purposeful excellence.*

My Life In Full by Indra Nooyi is an illuminating journey through the life and career of one of the world's most admired CEOs. Nooyi's memoir offers readers a firsthand account of her rise to prominence as the first woman of color and immigrant to lead a Fortune 50 company, PepsiCo. With grace, grit, and humor, she shares the triumphs and challenges she faced along the way.

From her upbringing in 1960s India to her tenure at Yale School of Management and eventual ascent to the top ranks of corporate leadership, Nooyi's narrative is both captivating and insightful. She provides an inside look at PepsiCo's transformation under her leadership, emphasizing her commitment to healthier products and environmental sustainability despite resistance.

What sets this memoir apart is Nooyi's candid discussion of the difficulties of balancing her demanding career with family responsibilities. She advocates for prioritizing the care ecosystem, paid leave, and work flexibility, making a compelling case for their importance in unlocking economic potential.

Generous, authoritative, and grounded in lived experience, My Life in Full is not just the story of a remarkable leader, but also a rallying cry for positive change in both business and society. Nooyi's memoir is a must-read for anyone seeking inspiration and guidance in navigating the complexities of modern leadership and life.

# A Journey Through High-Impact Leadership with

# MARC ROWLEY

## Adapting Leadership in Today's Dynamic Landscape

BY A.J. SOMER

In the intricate world of business leadership and organisational transformation, few voices resonate as profoundly as that of Marc Rowley, Founder of HIT Leadership Consulting. With over three decades of hands-on experience in leading teams and driving impactful change, Marc embodies a rare blend of practical wisdom and visionary foresight. His journey from the trenches of corporate dynamics to the helm of consultancy has been guided by an unwavering commitment to service excellence and a relentless pursuit of understanding human interactions.

In this exclusive interview with Entrepreneur Prime magazine, Marc Rowley offers insights into the genesis of HIT Leadership Consulting and the guiding principles that underpin its mission. His passion for service excellence led him to delve into the psychology of human behaviour, mindfulness, and the intricate dance between employee and customer engagement. It's a journey fuelled by a genuine desire to help people thrive, grounded in strong morals, ethics, and a high level of empathy.

At the heart of HIT Leadership Consulting's methodology lies the concept of Honesty, Integrity and Transparency (HIT), a holistic approach that transcends conventional leadership paradigms. Marc's diverse background, coupled with a relentless pursuit of knowledge and innovation, enables him to offer bespoke solutions tailored to each client's unique needs and challenges.

*Marc Rowley, Founder of HIT Leadership Consulting, epitomizes visionary leadership with a blend of wisdom and foresight, guiding transformative organizational change.*

*Marc Rowley shares his journey founding HIT Leadership Consulting, emphasising personalised strategies for leadership, employee, and customer engagement, driving sustainable growth.*

Central to HIT Leadership Consulting's ethos is the Discovery Stage, a meticulously designed process aimed at unravelling the intricacies of each organisation's DNA. Through this stage, Marc and his team delve deep into the operational, cultural, and leadership landscapes of their clients, paving the way for tailored solutions that drive sustainable growth and success.

In a dynamic business environment where priorities often compete for attention, Marc sheds light on the critical importance of prioritizing employee and customer engagement. By integrating engagement practices into the core operational frameworks of businesses, HIT Leadership Consulting ensures that these aspects become intrinsic to the company's DNA, fostering environments where both employees and customers thrive.

Marc also addresses common challenges in leadership engagement, offering insights into how coaching and training programs can empower leaders to navigate change and foster inclusive, resilient cultures. Through real-world success stories, he illustrates the tangible impact of HIT Leadership Consulting's approach on productivity, revenue, and brand reputation.

As businesses navigate the evolving landscape of remote and hybrid work arrangements, Marc discusses how HIT Leadership Consulting adapts its services to maintain a positive workplace culture and high levels of employee engagement. By emphasizing transparent communication, flexible policies, and digital collaboration tools, HIT Leadership Consulting ensures that organisations remain connected and resilient in the face of change.

Looking ahead, Marc shares his vision for the future of business leadership and engagement, foreseeing trends such as sustainability, AI, and continued evolution in remote work. With an unwavering commitment to continuous learning and adaptability, HIT Leadership Consulting stands poised to guide businesses towards success in an ever-changing world.

Marc Rowley's journey and insights serve as a beacon of inspiration for leaders seeking to navigate the complexities of modern business with integrity, empathy, and visionary leadership. Through HIT Leadership Consulting, Marc continues to shape the future of organisational transformation, one engagement at a time.

**What inspired you to start HIT Leadership Consulting, and how does your background contribute to your approach in guiding businesses towards growth and success?**

Inspiration and Background: The genesis of HIT Leadership Consulting was born out of a profound understanding of the myriad challenges businesses face in leadership and engagement, fuelled by over three decades of first-hand leadership experience. My journey through the ranks of small to large corporations instilled in me the critical importance of effective leadership, employee engagement, and customer satisfaction in achieving sustainable growth. The concept of HIT Leadership - Honesty, Integrity and Transparency was inspired by the recognition of

a gap in the market for a holistic approach to leadership that not only focuses on the foundational aspects of leading teams but also integrates advanced elements like mental resilience and political intelligence. My diverse background enables me to bring a comprehensive perspective to guiding businesses, blending practical leadership experience with innovative training methodologies to foster environments where both employees and leaders thrive.

**Could you walk us through the process of the Discovery Stage in your consulting services? How do you tailor your approach to each client's unique needs and challenges?**

Discovery Stage Process: At the heart of our consulting services lies the Discovery Stage, a meticulously designed process aimed at understanding the unique DNA of each client. This stage involves an in-depth analysis of the client's current operational, cultural, and leadership landscapes. Through interviews, surveys, and observational studies, we gather insights into the challenges and opportunities within the organisation. Tailoring our approach involves aligning our findings with the client's strategic objectives, ensuring that the solutions we propose are not only bespoke but also scalable and sustainable. This personalized methodology allows us to address specific pain points while positioning the company for long-term success.

**Employee engagement and customer experience are central to your consulting services. How do you ensure that businesses prioritize these aspects amidst their day-to-day operations, especially in today's dynamic business environment?**

Prioritising Employee and Customer Engagement: Ensuring that businesses maintain a focus

on employee engagement and customer experience amid their day-to-day operations requires a strategic approach. We integrate engagement practices into the core operational frameworks of the businesses we work with, making these aspects an intrinsic part of the company's DNA rather than standalone initiatives. By leveraging continuous improvement frameworks and embedding engagement metrics into performance management systems, businesses can monitor and adapt their strategies in real-time, ensuring they remain responsive to both employee and customer needs even in a dynamic business environment.

**In your experience, what are some common challenges businesses face when it comes to leadership engagement, and how do you address these challenges through your coaching and training programs?**

Challenges in Leadership Engagement: Common challenges in leadership engagement include a lack of alignment with the company's vision, inadequate communication skills, and difficulty in adapting to change. Our coaching and training programs address these issues by focusing on emotional intelligence, effective communication, and change management. By equipping leaders with the tools and insights to understand and motivate their teams, we foster a culture of inclusivity, resilience, and adaptability, thereby enhancing overall leadership engagement.

**Can you share a success story or example of a business that significantly improved its productivity and revenue after implementing your leadership engagement workshop or employee engagement training?**

Success Story: A testament to the efficacy of our approach is a mid-sized retail company that, after participating in our leadership engagement workshop, witnessed a remarkable turnaround. By implementing our strategies, the company saw a 40% increase in employee engagement scores within six months, which translated into a 25% growth in productivity and a significant uplift in revenue. This success story underscores the direct correlation between engaged leadership, motivated employees, and business performance.

**Customer engagement is vital for business success. How do you help businesses build personalized and meaningful customer experiences, and what measurable outcomes can they expect from investing in your customer engagement training program?**

Building Personalised Customer Experiences: Our approach to enhancing customer engagement centres on understanding the unique preferences and expectations of the customer base. We help businesses implement feedback mechanisms and customer journey mapping to tailor experiences that resonate with their customers. Investing in our customer engagement training program yields measurable outcomes, including increased customer loyalty, higher conversion rates, and enhanced brand reputation. These metrics not only signify the program's success but also highlight the substantial return on investment businesses can achieve by prioritizing customer engagement.

**With the rise of remote and hybrid work arrangements, how do you adapt your consulting services to help businesses maintain a positive workplace culture and high levels of employee engagement?**

Adapting to Remote and Hybrid Work: The shift towards remote and hybrid work models has necessitated a revaluation of traditional workplace culture and engagement strategies. Our consulting services have evolved to include digital transformation initiatives, remote leadership training, and virtual team-building activities designed to maintain a cohesive and engaging workplace culture. We emphasize the importance of transparent communication, flexible work policies, and digital collaboration tools to ensure that employees feel connected and valued, regardless of their physical work location.

**Looking ahead, what trends do you foresee in the realm of business leadership and employee/customer engagement, and how do you plan to evolve your consulting offerings to address these trends effectively?**

Future Trends and Adaptations: Looking ahead, we anticipate trends such as the increasing importance of sustainability and social responsibility, the rise of AI and machine learning in decision-making, and the continued evolution of remote work. To stay at the forefront, HIT Leadership Consulting plans to integrate these emerging trends into our offerings, focusing on developing leaders who are not only adept at navigating technological advancements but are also champions of ethical and sustainable business practices. Emphasizing continuous learning and adaptability, we aim to equip businesses to thrive in an ever-changing landscape, ensuring they remain competitive and resilient.

In summary, HIT Leadership Consulting's approach is rooted in a deep understanding of the intricacies of leadership and engagement, refined through decades of experience. Our personalized and forward-thinking strategies are designed to address the unique challenges businesses face today, driving growth, productivity, and success through effective leadership and engagement practices.

PHOTO: *Marc Rowley: Empowering leaders, transforming organizations, and shaping the future of business with HIT Leadership Consulting.*

# Leading with 3SIXTY Vision: An Exclusive Interview with

# ROCKY ROMANELLA

## Insights on Leadership, Adaptation, and Customer-Centricity from a Seasoned CEO and Author

BY ACACIA BALDIE

*Rocky Romanella shares leadership insights emphasizing holistic approaches, adaptation, collaboration, customer-centricity, and personal growth, drawn from his diverse industry experience and bestselling book, Tighten The Lug Nuts.*

Entrepreneur Prime Magazine is privileged to present an exclusive interview with Rocky Romanella, a titan in the realms of leadership, business strategy, and organizational transformation. With a career spanning over 45 years, Rocky has left an indelible mark on industries ranging from supply chain and logistics to retail and telecommunications.

As the former CEO of The UPS Store, Rocky orchestrated one of the most monumental rebranding endeavours in franchising history, reshaping the landscape of the retail shipping and business services market. His innovative approach didn't stop there; he spearheaded UPS's foray into the healthcare industry, pioneering a customer-centric mantra: "It's a patient, not a package.®"

Now at the helm of 3SIXTY Management Services, LLC, Rocky continues to inspire leaders worldwide with his concept of "3SIXTY Leadership," advocating for a holistic approach that encompasses every facet of business and personal development.

*Rocky Romanella epitomizes visionary leadership, blending wisdom, integrity, and resilience to transform industries and inspire leaders globally.*

In this insightful interview, Rocky delves into key principles and strategies essential for navigating today's dynamic business environment. From fostering collaboration and motivation within teams to advocating for a customer-centric ethos, his wisdom resonates deeply with leaders seeking to thrive amidst uncertainty and change.

Join us as Rocky Romanella shares invaluable insights gleaned from a lifetime of leadership, offering a roadmap for success rooted in integrity, resilience, and unwavering commitment to excellence.

**You emphasize the importance of "3SIXTY Leadership", which involves leading in every direction. Could you elaborate on what this concept means to you and how it shapes your approach to leadership?**

Its concept means leaving no aspect of business behind. A successful leadership team won't find and create success if they don't focus on the business and the employee as a whole. This means as a leader you need to focus on everything from changing the business landscape, and developing strategies, tactics, and metrics to drive desired results, as well as, personal development: time management, self-sabotaging behaviour (like procrastination and distraction), finding clarity, decision making, and getting into action. It also means when a problem arises, finding the answers from within yourselves and the organization.

**In today's fast-paced business environment, adaptation is key. How do you advise leaders and organizations to navigate change effectively, especially when faced with unexpected disruptions like those seen in recent times?**

When there are unexpected disruptions, you have three choices: lead, follow or get out of the way. Unexpected disruptions are what sets apart the good companies and the great companies. During challenging times, and periods of rapid changes, good companies and leaders view consistency as their high-water mark. Great companies and leaders emerge from these difficulties a stronger and more competitive company positioned for great success – like a phoenix. In many cases good companies are in a maintenance mode and are happy with relative results, whereas great companies and leaders are highly motivated with a strong commitment to growing and having exponential results. In the event an unimaginable detour arises, good companies will manage tactfully and consistently. Great companies will be the architects of their own destinies. They will decide; What are the steps we will take to build back our company? What will our brand stand for in this evolving time? And what will our brand promise be? Good companies rely on what they know to do, Great companies prepare for what they will need to do.

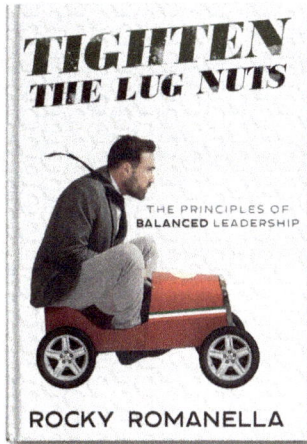

*Unlock the secrets to success with Tighten the Lug Nuts: The Principles of Balanced Leadership by Rocky Romanella. This #1 Best-Selling Leadership Book offers a roadmap for achieving greatness in your career and business. Romanella's insights, drawn from years of experience and real-world examples, illuminate the path from ordinary to extraordinary leadership. Learn how to cultivate a winning mindset, build effective teams, and maximize productivity. A must-read for anyone aspiring to reach new heights in leadership and beyond.*

**Your experience includes leading teams in diverse industries. What strategies do you find most effective in fostering collaboration, motivation, and high performance within teams, particularly in challenging or competitive markets?**

First and foremost, Leadership is not a passive duty, it is an active responsibility. In other words, get out from behind your desk and walk around. You must have personal integrity, live your word; establish open, candid, trusting and respectful relationships at all levels and especially with your direct reports. When you treat all people inside and outside of your organization fairly and respectfully, you will see others bring their own discipline, hard work, and enthusiasm to work each day. True empowerment is when people discipline themselves.

Also, as a leader you must be able to handle differences in work styles effectively when working with co-workers and capitalizing on strengths of others on a team to get work done even when they are your peers. It will be important to anticipate potential conflicts and address them directly and effectively before they become a problem or distraction.

**Customer satisfaction is a priority for any successful business. How do you advocate for a customer-centric approach within organizations, and what steps can leaders take to ensure that their teams consistently deliver exceptional customer experiences?**

One of the biggest differentiators between good and great is the superior customer experience that is provided on a consistent basis. During every customer interaction, your reputation is on the line. Remember, as a leader, your customers are also the people in your care and supervision. Whether on the phone, in person, or via electronic communication, genuinely interact and connect with customers; ensure

a positive experience and exceed expectations. Anyone who comes in contact with a customer needs to actively listen to a customer's needs and consistently demonstrate to customers that they are in tune with their needs and are operating in their best interest. Never underestimate the power of your brand and your reputation in the marketplace. Wherever your strategic path takes you, know that your brand and trustworthiness is your highest honour.

**Can you share more about the significance of the title Tighten the Lug Nuts and how it reflects the principles of balanced leadership outlined in your book?**

The phrase, "Tighten The Lug Nuts," simply means, do not allow important things to become urgent. You can only manage a few urgent things at a time so do not let important items that can be quickly taken care of become urgent, they can and will overwhelm you. Urgent problems often become what people refer to as "fire" in the workplace. It's okay to have urgent situations once in a while. But often, these dire circumstances are created when people don't "tighten their lug nuts." It may be a common pattern occurring within the same department or caused by the same leader. The frustrating thing for many employees is that if the problem were taken care of when it was important, it wouldn't get to a state of urgency. Because as things move from "important" to "urgent," people begin to get overwhelmed and make decisions that may be rash or add to the fire.

The key to tightening the lug nuts as a leader is to recognize when an important problem does arise. Then stop and react quickly to establish a course of action that will drive desired results. Create a way forward, and implement a measurement process to monitor progress.

In urgent situations there are three important questions you

can ask your team:

If we had taken care of this sooner, when it was important, would it have risen to this level of urgency? What role did I play in causing this to become urgent? And how can we make sure this doesn't happen again moving forward?

**Your journey from a part-time package loader to President of The UPS Store and UPS Supply Chain Solutions is quite remarkable. What were some of the key principles or strategies you employed along the way that you believe contributed most to your success?**

1. You can disagree, but you should not be disagreeable or disrespectful.

2. Be humble and learn everything you can about your job, and then learn some more

3. Recognize it is what you do when no one is watching that counts most because it's the true measure of your character.

4. Don't let your highs get too high and your lows get too low

5. Don't always stop at the first right answer

**In your book, you emphasize the importance of mindset and attitude in distinguishing successful leaders. Could you elaborate on what this mindset entails and how aspiring leaders can cultivate it to achieve their career goals?**

You have a responsibility to yourself and to others to use your best judgment, weigh your options carefully, and make the right decisions—even if they're not the most favourable or popular, even when no one is watching! When you do that, you honour yourself and your values. Wherever your path takes you, know that your trustworthiness is your highest honour. For if you are a trusted leader, others will believe in your vision, mission, and values and will trust in you enough to follow you. That will be your legacy. As a person your core beliefs are not what you would like them to be, but rather what lives and breathes in you as a person.

# Unveiling the World with
# BORIS KESTER
## Exploring Cultures, Unexpected Encounters, and the Essence of Global Exploration

Boris Kester, global adventurer, shares insights from visiting all 193 countries: surprising encounters, risky moments, and advice for aspiring travellers. His books capture the essence of exploration and curiosity.

*Boris Kester's global odyssey: exploring cultures, risking encounters, embracing transformation. From travel tales to literary endeavors, curiosity endures.*

In a world where borders are not just lines on a map but markers of identity, Boris Kester defies conventional boundaries with his insatiable thirst for exploration. His journey is not merely about tallying passport stamps but about unraveling the intricate threads that weave together the fabric of humanity itself. Through his remarkable odyssey, Boris has not only traversed the physical landscapes of 193 countries but has delved deep into the cultural tapestry of our planet, leaving behind a trail of stories that inspire and captivate.

In our exclusive interview with Boris Kester for Entrepreneur Prime magazine, we embark on a voyage beyond borders, guided by his unparalleled experiences and profound insights. From the remote corners of Kiribati to the vibrant streets of Gabon, Boris shares tales of unexpected encounters and daring escapades, offering a glimpse into the unpredictable essence of global exploration.

As Boris reflects on his encounters and challenges, he unveils the transformative power of travel, urging aspiring adventurers to embrace the unknown with open minds and open hearts. His words resonate with the wisdom gained from years of traversing continents, reminding us to slow down, savor the moments, and immerse ourselves in the beauty of our world and its people.

Beyond the confines of his expeditions, Boris invites us into the realm of storytelling, where the challenge lies in distilling a lifetime of adventures into the pages of his acclaimed book, *The Long Road to Cullaville*. Yet, amidst his literary pursuits and ongoing adventures, Boris remains anchored in the boundless allure of discovery, beckoning us to join him on a journey that transcends borders and defies expectations.

Join us as we embark on an extraordinary odyssey with Boris Kester, a modern-day explorer whose wanderlust knows no bounds and whose stories illuminate the vastness of our world and the endless possibilities that lie ahead.

**What was the most surprising or unexpected encounter you had during your travels to all 193 countries?**

Traveling in Kiribati (in the Pacific), I met a local guy who asked me where I was from. I told him, and since he didn't know the Netherlands, I said it was close to Germany, France, and the United Kingdom. He then asked me how many hours it would take me to get to Germany by boat. I was surprised, and explained that you take a car, train, or bicycle to

get

*Boris Kester's global journey transcends borders, embracing diverse cultures, unpredictable encounters, and the transformative power of exploration and storytelling.*

across the border. He didn't understand this, and then asked me how much time it would take me to reach France by boat. Again, I told him that you can get to France by land and that there are no boats linking the two countries. I decided not to tell him that there's even another country, Belgium, separating the two. I went on to

*The Long Road to Cullaville - Boris Kester's captivating memoir chronicles his extraordinary adventures across the globe.*

tell him that I could travel all the way to China without ever taking a ship, and crossing many borders. He looked at me with a blank stare.

At first, I wondered how he could not know that most countries in Europe share land borders. Then, it dawned on me. This guy was from a nation of islands, in a region of islands. The island defines your identity. Bigger nations in the region are island nations, too: Philippines, Japan, New Zealand, Australia, Indonesia. Islands are clearly marked entities by nature. It put my whole project of visiting every country in a new perspective: I realized that borders are a human invention.

**Can you share a particularly challenging or risky situation you encountered during your quest to visit every country?**

When I refused to pay a bribe at a checkpoint in Gabon, and the (drunk) official didn't give me my passport, we ended up in a physical fight over the document. I was extremely fortunate that at exactly that moment, a convoy of vehicles passed by. The Minister of Justice happened to be in one of the vehicles, and he summoned both of us to talk to him. He made a call, and within twenty minutes, several police officers arrived. They sorted out the situation. I have always wondered what would have happened in case that minister wouldn't have passed by. Destiny (or sheer luck) is an important factor in both travel and life, and as such

one of the themes of my book.

**What advice would you give to aspiring travellers who want to embark on a similar journey to visit all the countries in the world?**

I have two pieces of advice for them. First: leave your preconceptions at home. Embark on your journeys with an open mind, a curious mind, in which everything is possible. Be open to be surprised, and you will soon find out what an incredibly beautiful world we live in with equally beautiful people (most of the time). If you manage to travel this way, your travels will probably be the best teacher of life you ever had.

Secondly, I would tell all aspiring travellers to take it easy, and to take their time. I see quite a few travellers rushing through the world, ticking off countries, and I honestly don't see the sense of it. Enjoy your travels, take your time to get to know a country, to connect with people, to absorb what is happening around you. Travel is not competition, and if you don't make it to visit every country, that's perfectly fine.

**How did writing your books differ from sharing your travel experiences on your website? Did you find it challenging to condense your adventures into book form?**

I have shared my travel adventures since 25 years through my website traveladventures. org. Soon after visiting my last country, and completing my goal to visit every country in the world, I realized that the most exciting stories were hard or impossible to share through short stories on the internet. It was obvious that the best way to do so would be through a book. Anyway, it had been a child's dream to one day publish a

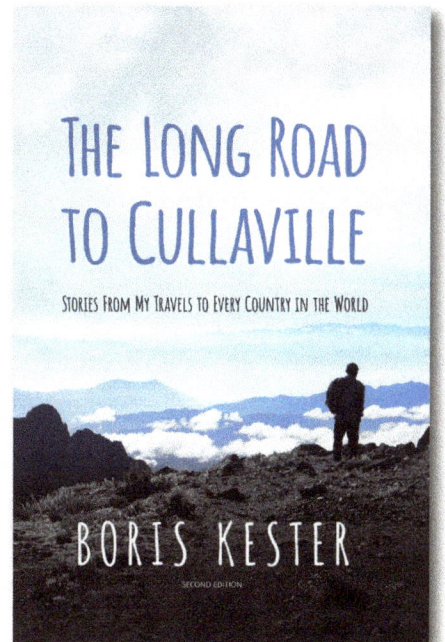

# THE LONG ROAD TO CULLAVILLE

STORIES FROM MY TRAVELS TO EVERY COUNTRY IN THE WORLD

# BORIS KESTER

SECOND EDITION

book. Indeed, I loved the process of writing. I had all the space I needed to tell my stories, and I worked hard to turn my travel adventures into literary words, as opposed to the internet where I write more like a reportage.

**Now that you have visited all countries in the world, what's next?**

I may have visited every country in the world, the main driving force behind my travels - curiosity - is still very much alive. I am still travelling like before, but without a clear goal in mind which, in a way, is liberating. I have a long list of places I want to visit. Through other travellers, I often get new ideas for places to visit. I do find, however, that I am avoiding touristy places. I am travelling to places where few people go, discovering obscure sites, enjoying breathtaking nature, while wondering why most people never get there.

**Can we expect a second book from you?**

Definitely! Shortly after my first book came out, I started writing my second one. First of all because many readers asked me for a sequel as they enjoyed the first book so much. Secondly, because I loved the writing process, and thirdly because I still have many more stories to share. My goal is to publish the second book in 2024. Besides, I am working on a third book as well, together with another traveller.

# Women Leaders Share Their Best Advice With The Next Generation

*Leading the Way: Insights from Wells Fargo's Female Powerhouses*

Setting and reaching goals is never easy, and if you're a woman, you will likely face additional challenges on the path to achieving your dreams. But in the realm of banking, five remarkable women are breaking barriers and reshaping the industry. As honorees of American Banker's "Most Powerful Women in Banking," these leaders from Wells Fargo are not just paving the way; they're sharing invaluable advice with the next generation of female leaders.

### TRACY KERRİNS: STICK TO YOUR GOALS

Tracy Kerrins, Wells Fargo's head of technology, knows a thing or two about navigating obstacles. As one of the few women in a top tech role at a major American bank, Kerrins emphasizes the importance of persistence. "Stick to your goals, even when obstacles emerge, and rely on those who are truly invested in your success," she advises. Kerrins' strategic mindset keeps her ahead in a rapidly evolving tech landscape, where she's driving innovations to enhance the banking experience.

### KRISTY FERCHO: CULTIVATE CURIOSITY

For Kristy Fercho, leading transformation in banking is not just a job—it's a mission. As head of diverse segments, representation, and inclusion at Wells Fargo, Fercho underscores the value of curiosity. "Be excellent at your job. Be curious. And most importantly: Be your authentic self," she advocates. Her commitment to diversity and inclusion fuels positive change within Wells Fargo and beyond.

### ELLEN PATTERSON: LIFT OTHERS AS YOU RISE

Ellen Patterson, Wells Fargo's general counsel, credits her success to the collective effort of her team. Leading over 1,200 legal professionals, Patterson believes in the power of collaboration and mentorship. "Be great at what you're doing, and actively look for ways to be helpful to those around you," she advises. Patterson's approach fosters a culture of support and excellence within her team.

### TANYA SANDERS: INNOVATE SOLUTIONS

As head of Wells Fargo's auto division, Tanya Sanders combines banking expertise with a passion for problem-solving. With a background in mechanical engineering, Sanders sees challenges as opportunities for innovation. "There is incredible power in forging new and inclusive solutions," she asserts. Sanders encourages future leaders to collaborate and drive positive change for all.

### KARA MCSHANE: MASTER THE ART OF COMMUNICATION

Kara McShane, head of Wells Fargo's commercial real estate division, understands the significance of effective communication in business. "Learn how to communicate clearly, concisely and confidently in order to be effective," she advises. McShane's emphasis on communication skills underscores their role in leadership success.

Whether you're a student, a recent graduate, or a seasoned professional, the wisdom shared by these outstanding women leaders can guide you through challenges and propel you towards success. By embracing their lessons, you can chart your own path to leadership and make a lasting impact in the banking industry and beyond.

# Business Owners Are Optimistic as Economic Conditions Improve

What a difference a year makes. New research finds that small- and mid-sized business owners are increasingly optimistic about economic conditions and the prospects for their own businesses.

According to PNC's Spring 2024 Economic Outlook Survey, nearly 80% of business owners surveyed feel optimistic about conditions for their business over the next six months -- up from 60% a year ago.

This optimism likely stems from an improving outlook for the economy as a whole as inflation pressures and recession fears appear to be easing. A majority of those surveyed (55%) said they are highly optimistic about the national economy -- a dramatic increase from the 26% who felt that way in the spring of 2023. Even more (63%) said they are highly optimistic about their local economy -- more than double the reading from a year ago.

The uptick in optimism for the economy mirrors PNC's revised outlook for 2024, which shifts away from a predicted recession to a forecast of slow growth. PNC chief economist Gus Faucher said he expects the Federal Reserve will begin cutting interest rates later this year as inflation continues to ease.

"Business owners continue to feel confident that good days are ahead," Faucher said. "This time around though, the economy is seen as a supporting factor to that optimism instead of a limitation."

## Calming Inflation

Easing inflation pressures are among the biggest factors reported in the survey. Last spring, 55% of respondents reported that they expected to raise prices in the ensuing six months -- that dropped to 47% this round. Similarly, 40% expect prices from suppliers to increase over the next six months, that's down from 47% last spring.

Inflation overall has been gradually easing since a mid-2022 high of 9% -- its highest level since the 1980s. By January 2024, inflation was reported at 3.1%, with continued easing projected in the months ahead. Still, inflation remains above its pre-pandemic pace and Faucher says more progress is needed before the Fed likely cuts rates later in 2024.

"We've come a long way from 2022, as supply chain issues driven by the pandemic have largely dissipated," Faucher said. "But more progress will probably be necessary before we can expect the Fed to start easing rates."

## Labor Challenges Easing

One such challenge has been the tight labor market, which has made hiring difficult for business leaders. Consistent with PNC's Fall 2023 survey, respondents say the lack of overall applicants remains their primary hiring issue. Respondents cite lack of experience (22%) and high salary/benefit and flexibility requirements (9%) as other barriers.

The nationwide unemployment rate for January 2024 was 3.7% -- below what is considered "full employment" in the U.S. economy. Faucher said he expects the shortage of available labor to ease as consumer demand softens and the effect of slower job growth across the economy becomes more visible.

Despite the trend across the broader U.S. landscape, few survey respondents anticipate workforce reductions over the next six months. Only 4% report anticipating a reduction, while 74% expect no change to their workforce numbers and 21% project an increase in their workforce over the next half of the year.

"Employers have been under pressure despite the improving conditions because the economy has been at or near full employment for an extended period," Faucher said. "We expect some slack in the labor market in the coming months, which will likely further ease inflation." (StatePoint)

# Unravelling Urban Dynamics
# A Conversation with
# Ramon Gras Alomà

In the bustling landscape of urban development, where innovation meets the timeless challenge of sustainable design, one name stands out: Ramon Gras Alomà. An architect of urban futures, Ramon's journey is a testament to the power of interdisciplinary vision and unwavering dedication to reshaping our cities for the better.

Ramon Gras Alomà, adorned with degrees from BarcelonaTech, MIT, and Harvard, embodies a rare fusion of academia and entrepreneurship. As a City Science and Urban Design researcher at Harvard and the Co-founder of Aretian Urban Analytics and Design, his work transcends conventional boundaries, delving into the intricate nexus of technology, economics, and human flourishing within urban environments.

In his recent endeavour, "City Science: Performance Follows Form," Ramon offers a compelling narrative of urban dynamics, unpacking the hidden causal mechanisms that underpin the success or failure of cities in an era marked by technological revolution. This pioneering work serves as a beacon guiding urban planners, policymakers, and architects toward more informed, sustainable practices.

In our exclusive interview with Ramon Gras Alomà for Entrepreneur Prime magazine, we delve into the genesis of his entrepreneurial journey and the challenges encountered along the way. From the inception of Aretian to the validation of their ground-breaking methodologies, Ra-

*"Ramon Gras Alomà, urban visionary and co-founder of Aretian, blends academia and entrepreneurship to reshape urban landscapes. Their groundbreaking methodologies promise transformative impact in sustainable urban design."*

mon shares insights into the intricate dance between innovation and pragmatism in the realm of urban design.

Reflecting on the inception of Aretian, Ramon unveils a journey fuelled by a relentless pursuit of understanding urban complexities. His collaboration with Jeremy Burke birthed a methodology grounded in evidence-based complex systems, offering a novel lens to measure and evaluate urban success. Through empirical validation and accolades from prestigious institutions, Aretian swiftly garnered recognition, laying the foundation for transformative impact.

At the heart of Ramon's vision lies a profound commitment to societal well-being, encapsulated in Aretian's unique approach. With a diverse team of trailblazers and a steadfast focus on addressing critical urban challenges, Aretian stands as a beacon of innovation in the urban development landscape.

For aspiring entrepreneurs, Ramon offers sage advice rooted in the primacy of people and purpose. With a keen eye on the horizon, Aretian is poised to unveil its latest endeavour: a three-dimensional City Digital Twin.

This revolutionary tool promises to revolutionize urban development, offering a scalable solution to navigate the complexities of modern cities.

As we navigate the urban tapestry of the future, Ramon Gras Alomà and Aretian Urban Analytics and Design emerge as guiding lights, illuminating a path towards sustainable, vibrant cities. Join us as we embark on a journey through the corridors of innovation and reimagine the cities of tomorrow, one visionary step at a time.

## What inspired you to start your business?

In the Spring of 2018, I graduated from Harvard with a thesis on city science and urban design, aiming to inform sustainable development best practices in the face of the technology revolution driven by AI, automation, and robotics. The goal was to understand the deep, nontrivial causal mechanisms behind the success or failure of different cities and urban environments in order to create sustained prosperity cycles whilst raising the standard of living of citizens, in a context of high uncertainty in the global economy. My fellow co-founder

Jeremy Burke and I worked together on designing an evidence-based complex systems methodology to model in a visual and mathematical way cities, urban environments, and architectural spaces, hence allowing us to measure and evaluate their success by means of Key Performance Metrics, illuminating structural and global patterns, and extracting insights to inform successful urban design and economic development strategies tailored for each society, context, and moment. We empirically validated a series core hypotheses by modeling first the US territory, then the World, thus allowing for creating a new model able to provide highly valuable recommendations and inform decision-making when addressing complex urban challenges worldwide.

## What challenges did you find at the beginning of your journey and how did you overcome them?

We designed a new methodology (city science) for a early stage, nascent industry (city digital twins) in a new sector (smart cities), with a new team, so the first challenge was to prove the applicability of the new solution, and its ability to illustrate causal mechanisms, and to provide highly valuable insights that can raise the quality of decision making in urban design, architecture, civil engineering, economic development and real estate-related projects. The market tends to be sceptical about new solutions, and rather conservative. Thankfully, the more talented and brilliant our potential customers are, the more they understand and visua-

*Ramon Gras Alomà, co-founder of Aretian Urban Analytics and Design, illuminates the future of urban innovation through interdisciplinary vision and pioneering methodologies"*

lize the value of our contributions. A series of academic publications, and white paper reports, such as the Atlas of Innovation Districts, published in 2019 and announced by MIT Technology Review, provided visibility to our methods and grounded their scientific credibility. Happily, our team and projects received some awards from the Harvard Graduate School of Design (Excellence in Design Award), Harvard Office for Sustainability, BostInno, and the CogX / British academy for AI (Sustainable Cities and Communities Award), among others, as well as an interview at the Harvard Magazine contributed to disseminate the knowledge advances achieved by embracing this new methodology, and that helped us get our first clients in Boston, New York, and abroad.

### How did you get the idea for your business and why did you think it would work?

We identified in our own professional practice in architecture, civil engineering and urban design a methodological gap that was hindering the ability for urban designers and city planners to address a series of key questions, such as how to address the needs of a specific community, and align aesthetics, functionality, and sustainability to create attractive and thriving communities. We drew inspiration from prior authors that we admire like Louis Durand, Ildefons Cerdà, Geoffrey West, Évariste Galois, Euler, or Eratosthenes, and their intuitions helped us conceive our core hypothesis, assumptions, and a vision of how the urban form, economic systems, and social dynamics can be modeled to describe mathematically how cities operative and what are the key ingredients and dynamics behind the success, economic dynamism, appeal, attractiveness and desirability of any human settlement around the globe. After endless brainstorming sessions and modeling efforts, the city science model was very robust, and provided us with the types of answers we wanted to address.

### What kind of research did you do before you started?

We developed a thorough market research study to understand the needs of our potential client base across sectors such as urban design, city planning, economic development policymaking, real estate, and finance sectors: there really was an urgent need for more sophisticated ways of informing decision making processes for critical urban development projects . Besides, our work on urban innovation communities through the Atlas of Innovation Districts and rural development needs such as the Aretian Agritechnology Campuses helped us ascertain the challenges that public administration and private investors constantly face when facing development challenges.

### What motivates you to keep going? What makes your business unique?

The vision and methodology that we have designed is grounded on a fertile land and we continually advance our methods and solutions. We have a fantastic team, composed of highly talented, motivated and principled professionals, and we constantly strive for pushing the boundaries of the frontier of knowledge, aiming to provide a social service that can potentially have an immense impact on the quality of life, personal, and professional prospects of citizens worldwide. Such a compelling challenge is highly stimulating, and keeps a cohesive team and strengthens a shared ethos.

### What advice would you give to someone who is trying to become an entrepreneur?

I would encourage them to primarily focus on the people, the team, and the social challenge they are addressing. A healthy, supportive work environment is critical for the success of any company, and the wellbeing of its employees.

### What plans do you have for the future?

We are completing the design of a three-dimensional City Digital Twin, including a user-friendly web-based interface, that allows for addressing critical urban development challenges (urban design, smart specialization, innovation and talent development, mobility and logistics, housing and space programming) by performing four types of analyses: (1) highly detailed territorial SWOT diagnostics, (2) goal identification, (3) scenario planning and simulation, and (4)

# How
# Heidi Ellert-McDermott
# Transformed Speechwriting with
# Innovation, Wit, and SpeechyAI

*Heidi Ellert-McDermott's Speechy revolutionizes speechwriting, born from a need for witty wedding speeches. Overcoming SEO challenges, Speechy offers diverse services, led by top-notch writers. Marketing through PR and a book, Speechy aims to expand with SpeechyAI, balancing entrepreneurship with life challenges.*

There are those that stand out not just for their innovation, but for their profound impact on personal moments and milestones. Enter Heidi Ellert-McDermott, a visionary entrepreneur who has reshaped the landscape of speechwriting with her brainchild, Speechy.

Heidi's journey into the realm of speechwriting was sparked by a cascade of wedding experiences where the speeches ranged from lackluster to cringe-worthy. Drawing from her background as a TV director and writer at the esteemed BBC, Heidi recognized an unmet need for modern, witty, and bespoke wedding speeches. Thus, Speechy was born.

What sets Speechy apart is not just its impeccable craftsmanship but also its adaptability. Evolving from its roots in wedding speeches, the company now offers a spectrum of services tailored to diverse needs and budgets. From speech edits to delivery coaching and even the groundbreaking SpeechyAI, Heidi's team ensures that every word resonates with authenticity and humor.

But the road to success was not without its challenges. Like any entrepreneur, Heidi faced the daunting task of navigating uncharted territory, from understanding SEO to mastering the art of delegation. Yet, fueled by her unwavering passion and commitment to excellence, she persevered, propelling Speechy to global acclaim.

What truly distinguishes Speechy is the caliber of its team. Comprised of industry luminaries who have graced the stages of BBC comedy shows and penned jokes for renowned comedians, Speechy's writers bring unparalleled expertise and warmth to every project. It's this winning combination of talent and empathy that has earned Speechy accolades from publications like The Observer and The New York Times.

As Heidi looks toward the future, her sights are set on further revolutionising the world of speechwriting with SpeechyAI. Powered by artificial intelligence and honed by the wisdom of Heidi's team, SpeechyAI promises to redefine how we craft speeches for weddings, businesses, and celebrations alike.

In the midst of her entrepreneurial journey, Heidi acknowledges the perpetual quest for balance between work and life, a challenge she tackles with characteristic grace and determination. Yet, through it all, her unwavering dedication to her craft and her clients remains steadfast, ensuring that every speech crafted by Speechy is not just memorable but truly unforgettable.

Join us as we delve into the remarkable story of Heidi Ellert-McDermott and the transformative power of Speechy, where every word is crafted with care and every moment is imbued with laughter and love.

### How did you get the idea for your business and why did you think it would work?

In my early 30s I went to a succession of weddings where the speeches were variable to say the least. The brilliant ones added a wonderful moment to the day, but more often than not, the speeches were either awkward or dull. After sitting through a 40 min speech and seeing a trio of best men escorted away from the mic, I realised wedding speakers might appreciate the help for professional speechwriters.

Having worked in the TV industry, I had lots of contacts who I knew could work well with people and create truly unique and witty speeches for them. My team have worked on topical news quizzes and ghostwrite for renowned comedians, so wedding speakers now have access to truly great writers at a reasonable cost.

Over the years, we've developed our offering so in response to our clients varying needs, ability and budgets. We now also offer...

• A speech edit service (where clients send their first draft and we make it better)

- Delivery coaching (having directed TV presenters for over a decade, I know the dos and don't of presenting)

- Speech templates – (cheap, fast turnaround option)

- SpeechyAI (combining our expertise with Artificial Intelligence)

### What challenges did you find at the beginning of your journey and how did you overcome them?

Having never run my own business, I was completely ignorant about everything, other than the speechwriting and setting up a strong team!

The biggest learning curve has been understanding SEO as all our business is done online. We are a global business that offers both bespoke services and e-commerce products and we market to a wide variety of demographics (from best men in Australia wanting a bespoke speech, to a mother of the groom in the States wanting a simple speech template) so understanding our keywords and focussing our targeting has been key to our growth.

### What makes your business unique?

Without a doubt, the quality of the Speechy team. They really are top of their game; writing for a range of BBC topical comedy shows, appearing in panel shows and ghostwriting for world-renowned comedians. They are also genuinely lovely people to work with and are excellent at building strong relationships with our clients.

### What advice would you give to someone who is trying to become an entrepreneur?

It's not easy! Everything takes longer than you hope and costs a lot more too.

There's no silver bullet, and not much downtime in the initial years. There's lots of blood, sweat and tears and running your own business can be tough. But, as long as you know you're providing a great service or product, the effort feels worth it.

At Speechy as offer a delight guarantee because we want all our customers and clients to love working with us. I personally

couldn't cope if they didn't! I care too much!

### How did you market your business?

Because we offer such an unusual service and we have a lot of expertise, I've found it relatively easy to get good PR. We've been featured everywhere from The Telegraph to Forbes. I've also appeared on Radio 4's Women's Hour and BBC Sounds 'Best Men' podcast.

We don't pay for any editorial features; we simply supply interesting and entertaining content.

Due to our growing reputation as the go-to speech experts, the fantastic Little, Brown Publishers released my book, 'The Modern Couple's Guide to Wedding Speeches' last year. Great how-to book, and great publicity too!

### What plans do you have for the future?

Our aim this year is to market SpeechyAI – https://www.speechy.com/product/speechyai/. We're confident it's a game-changer.

SpeechyAI utilises the power of Artificial Intelligence and the Speechy team's expertise to create wedding speeches that are funny, meaningful, and memorable. It's fun to use and affordable.

We'll be constantly improving it as the tech develops and we're also hoping to extend its ability beyond wedding speeches to business and celebration speeches too.

Exciting times ahead!

### What's the biggest challenge of being an entrepreneur?

Having a work-life balance. (Still not quite mastered that one!)

Important to be able to delegate.

I've also learnt not to attempt all marketing routes, and instead concentrate on the few that have proven to work for us. It's impossible to master all marketing options – especially with so many social media channels, as well as PPC, mailing lists, SEO, and PR to consider.

*"Heidi Ellert-McDermott revolutionises speechwriting with Speechy, offering bespoke, witty speeches. From weddings to celebrations, her team, backed by SpeechyAI, crafts unforgettable moments with innovation and expertise."*

# A Tapestry of Colours and Textures Promoting Greek Magic Worldwide

*OLIA Scarves, founded by Olympia Theofanopoulou, combines Greek heritage with modern design, sourcing silk from Soufli. Meticulously crafted, each piece reflects Greece's essence, aiming for global recognition.*

BY A.J. SOMER | LONDON

In the bustling heart of Athens lies a brand that seamlessly blends the essence of art, tradition, and luxury into exquisite wearable pieces. OLIA Scarves, founded by Olympia Theofanopoulou, stands as a testament to the rich tapestry of Greek culture and heritage, woven intricately into each silk scarf and pareo. As we delve into the story behind OLIA Scarves, we uncover a journey marked by passion, innovation, and a deep-rooted commitment to craftsmanship.

At the core of OLIA Scarves lies the vision to transform art into wearable masterpieces. Inspired by her love for photography and a chance encounter with locally produced silk in Northern Greece, Olympia embarked on a quest to marry her artistic pursuits with the timeless allure of silk fabric. What began as a spark of inspiration during a visit to the historic town of Soufli evolved into a flourishing venture that celebrates Greece's artistic legacy while embracing modern design aesthetics.

Olympia's background in Archaeological Conservation and Museum Studies, acquired at London's prestigious Institute of Archaeology, served as the foundation for her venture into the world of luxury fashion. With a keen eye for detail honed through years of studying and preserving artworks from around the globe, she brings a unique perspective to the design process at OLIA Scarves.

Each piece is meticulously crafted to capture the spontaneity and authenticity of her art photographs, ensuring that every scarf or pareo tells a story of its own.

Sourcing the purest silk from Soufli, a town steeped in silk-producing traditions dating back to Byzantine times, OLIA Scarves pays homage to Greece's rich heritage. The synergy between locally sourced silk and contemporary artistry not only elevates the quality of the products but also fosters sustainable practices within the European silk industry. By promoting two of Soufli's finest silk qualities, Crepe de Chine and Crepe Satin, OLIA Scarves stands as a beacon of ethical fashion, championing the revival of traditional craftsmanship.

As OLIA Scarves sets its sights on the global stage, aspirations of collaboration and innovation loom large on the horizon. With a successful debut at the Pure London & JATC Event, the brand garnered international acclaim, paving the way for future collaborations with artists and companies worldwide. Through its kaleidoscopic array of colours and textures, OLIA Scarves aims to transport a piece of Greece's magic to every corner of the globe, encapsulating the essence

**ADORNED IN ELEGANCE:**: *Models showcase OLIA Scarves, each a masterpiece fusing art and tradition. From Greece's rich heritage to modern design, these scarves captivate with every fold.*

PHOTOS BY KATERINA CHEILADAKI

*Olympia Theofanopoulou, a visionary blending heritage with innovation, epitomizes artistry and dedication. Through OLIA Scarves, her passion illuminates, weaving tales of Greek culture and luxury with impeccable craftsmanship.*

of its islands, seascapes, and cultural heritage.

Join us as we embark on a journey through the world of OLIA Scarves, where art becomes adornment, tradition meets innovation, and luxury finds its truest expression in the embrace of Greek silk.

### What inspired the creation of OLIA Scarves?

The founder, Olympia Theofanopoulou, was inspired during a visit to Soufli in Northern Greece, where she encountered locally produced silk. Impressed by its quality, she envisioned combining her art photographs with this luxurious material.

### How did Olympia Theofanopoulou's background influence the founding of OLIA Scarves?

- Olympia studied Archaeological Conservation and Museum Studies in London, which provided her with opportunities to visit art galleries and museums worldwide. Her studies and profession in conservation, coupled with her passion for photography, influenced her attention to detail and the unique design of OLIA Scarves.

### Where does OLIA Scarves source its silk from, and what is its significance?

OLIA Scarves sources its silk from Soufli, a small town in Northeastern Greece known for its historical significance in silk production. Soufli's climate and silk-producing traditions contribute to the superior quality of the silk, which is attributed to the silkworms feeding on sykamore tree leaves.

### What is the process involved in creating a silk scarf or pareo at OLIA Scarves?

The process involves several stages, including photograph selection, processing, colour testing, digital printing, fixing, drying, cutting, and finishing. Attention to detail ensures that each item combines the artistic elements of the photographs with the unique qualities of Greek silk.

### What are OLIA Scarves' future aspirations and collaboration plans?

OLIA Scarves aims to showcase Greece's cultural heritage and natural beauty through its products, with aspirations to expand globally and collaborate with artists and companies worldwide. Their scarves feature details and fragments of the Greek landscape, capturing small miracles often overlooked.

### Can you describe OLIA Scarves' experience at the Pure London & JATC Event?

The Pure London & JATC Event provided OLIA Scarves with their first exposure to the international market, offering invaluable insights and attracting visitors from various countries. The experience was enhanced by the publication of an article in the UK Entrepreneur Prime Magazine.

### How does OLIA Scarves maintain its focus on quality and authenticity?

OLIA Scarves ensures that its photographs convey spontaneity and authenticity, avoiding stylization. Attention to detail extends beyond technique to combine artistic elements with the unique qualities of Greek silk, resulting in luxury items that bestow beauty and elegance.

### What role does photography play in the creation of OLIA Scarves?

Photography is a fundamental aspect of OLIA Scarves, with founder Olympia Theofanopoulou's passion for art photography driving the brand's creation. The photographs, mainly drawn from Greece's rich history and natural treasures, are transformed into wearable luxury items, adding an intangible, ethereal essence to the scarves.

# Navigating the Future
# Dr. Terry McIvor's
# Vision for PNLPsy™ and Mental Health Support

*"Dr. Terry Mcivor, founder of IGH3P®, pioneers PNLPsy™, integrating NLP, psychology, and neuroscience. Empirical validation and ethical integrity define his approach, shaping the future of coaching and mental health support globally."*

We had the privilege of interviewing with pioneering psychologist Dr. Terry McIvor, President and Founder of the International Guild of Hypnotherapy, NLP, and 3 Principles Practitioners and Trainers (IGH3P®), to discuss his ground-breaking work in Pathophysiological Neuro Linguistic Psychology (PNLPsy™).

As an academic leader with expertise spanning neuroscience, psychiatric psychology, and empirical research, Dr. McIvor has dedicated his career to advancing the psychological sciences. Through his innovative integration of neuro-linguistic programming, empirical psychology, and neuroscience, Dr. McIvor is spearheading the development of PNLPsy™ - a revolutionary new framework poised to transform coaching, mentoring, and psychological therapies.

In this exclusive interview, Dr. McIvor shares with us the genesis of PNLPsy™, its immense potential to address pressing psychological needs, and his unwavering commitment to evidence-based practices and ethical integrity. We gain powerful insights into how PNLPsy™ leverages neuroplasticity for psychological change, sets new benchmarks for efficacy in coaching/mentoring, and promises to shape the future of psychological disciplines globally.

From his collaboration with elite specialists to his role leading IGH3P® in standardizing industry practices, it is clear this psychologist-turned-trailblazing-entrepreneur has set his sights on no less than a paradigm shift in his field. The implications of his pioneering work in PNLPsy™ cannot be overstated.

**Can you share the inspiration behind creating Pathophysiological Neuro Linguistic Psychology (PNLPsy™) and what led you to combine Neuro-Linguistic Programming (NLP), empirical psychology, and neuroscience in this innovative field?**

The development and continuing development of PNLPsy™ was and is quite a personal journey for me. As Chair of Psychology at Manipur International University, I've been in a unique position to observe the overlap and, sometimes, the gaps between various psychological disciplines. The idea was to create a discipline that not only bridges these gaps but also stands up to the rigours of empirical testing. With the university's resources, I'm excited about the prospect of conducting clinical trials to validate the efficacy of PNLPsy™ techniques.

**How do you envision PNLPsy™ contributing to the evolution of psychological sciences, and what unique advantages does it offer over traditional approaches?**

PNLPsy™ is set to make a significant mark on the psychological sciences. With the ability to conduct clinical trials at the university, we're not just theorising; we're proving. This evidence-based approach, combined with the practical aspects of NLP and the insights from neuroscience, offers a comprehensive framework that I believe will revolutionise how we understand and apply psychological practices.

**As the CEO of the International Guild of Hypnotherapy, NLP, and 3 Principles Practitioners and Trainers, how do you see PNLPsy™ influencing coaching and mentoring standards within the professional community?**

Leading the International Guild of Hypnotherapy, NLP, and 3 Principles Practitioners and Trainers has connected me with an extensive network of professionals. As we develop PNLPsy™, this network becomes invaluable, allowing us to set new benchmarks in coaching and mentoring. We're not just teaching; we're rigorously testing our methodologies to ensure they meet the highest standards of efficacy and ethics. While also working with the coaching and mentoring regulator.

**In your opinion, how does the integrative approach of PNLPsy™ enhance the effectiveness of psychological interventions, and what potential impact could it have on addressing psychological issues?**

The integrative approach of PNLPsy™, underpinned by solid research and clinical trials, naturally enhances the effectiveness of psychological interventions. We're not guessing here; we're applying scientifically validated techniques tailored to individual needs, ensuring our interventions are as impactful as possible.

**Could you provide examples of therapeutic approaches within PNLPsy™ that leverage neuroplasticity to address psychological challenges?**

At the heart of PNLPsy™ is

our focus on neuroplasticity, and being in a leadership position in a university department allows me to explore this through clinical research. We're developing therapeutic approaches that harness the brain's ability to rewire itself, offering hope and tangible results for those facing psychological challenges. The integration of sound psychological neurology and a sophisticated understanding of neuroplasticity into PNLPsy™ not only distinguishes it from traditional NLP but also ensures that it remains a dynamic, scientifically grounded discipline. As we continue to explore the complexity of the human brain, PNLPsy™ stands ready to adapt and incorporate these discoveries, promising a future of psychological practice that is both effective and deeply rooted in neuroscience.

### How does PNLPsy™ address the issue of pseudoscience in psychology, and what steps are taken to ensure that its methodologies are firmly grounded in evidence-based practices?

One of my key missions with PNLPsy™ is to clear the fog of pseudoscience that can sometimes cloud our field. Through rigorous clinical trials and a commitment to empirical evidence, we will ensure that PNLPsy™ stands as an example of a scientifically validated practice in psychology. We want to standardise the coaching industry, increasing standards and weeding out the cowboys and cowgirls.

### In terms of professional development, how does PNLPsy™ support coaches and mentors in accessing scientifically validated tools and techniques for their practice?

With the establishment of my accredited international professional body, IGH3P®, we're in a prime position to support coaches and mentors with tools and techniques that aren't just effective but are proven to be so. This is about elevating psychology, coaching, and mentoring practices to new heights, backed by solid research and ethical integrity.

### Ethics play a crucial role in PNLPsy™. Can you elaborate on the ethical principles guiding this discipline and how they contribute to maintaining integrity in psychological interventions?

Ethics are non-negotiable in PNLPsy™. As we advance this discipline, every step is taken with a deep sense of responsibility towards the individuals we serve. Our ethical guidelines are stringent, ensuring that every aspect of PNLPsy™, from research to practice, upholds the highest standards of integrity.

### As a leader in the field, how do you see PNLPsy™ shaping the future of coaching, mentoring, and psychological practices globally?:

With the resources and network at my disposal, I see PNLPsy™ as a pivotal force in shaping the future of psychological practices. We're not just creating a new discipline; we're setting a new standard that insists on empirical validation, ethical practice, and real-world efficacy.

### Can you share insights into your collaborative efforts with other well-being professional bodies and how these collaborations contribute to the ongoing development of PNLPsy™?

The development of PNLPsy™ is a collaborative endeavour. Working with a network of professional coaching, research, and accrediting organisations, we're not only advancing PNLPsy™ but also rigorously testing its therapeutic power. This collaborative approach ensures that PNLPsy™ is continually refined, validated, and aligned with the needs of those we aim to serve.

"

*Dr. Terry Mcivor, President and Founder of IGH3P®, leading the charge in revolutionizing psychological sciences with the innovative NLPsy™ approach"*

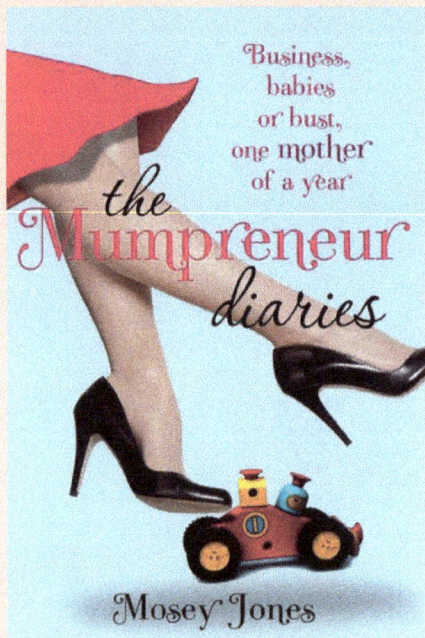

## THE MUMPRENEUR DIARIES
*By Mosey Jones*

## WHISKY BUSINESS
*By Elliot Fletcher*

## BUY, BUY BABY
*by Susan Gregory Thomas*

*Business, Babies or Bust - One Mother of a Year*

*Business, Babies or Bust - One Mother of a YearThe Mumpreneur Diaries* by Mosey Jones offers a refreshingly honest portrayal of the highs and lows of juggling motherhood and entrepreneurship. Jones' journey from the confines of a corporate commute to the unpredictable world of working from home with two young boys is both relatable and entertaining.

Jones' decision to embark on her mumpreneurial venture is sparked by a moment of clarity during her pregnant commute, where the allure of flexible hours and more time with her children becomes irresistible. However, as she delves into the world of running her own business while managing her family, she quickly discovers that the path to success is riddled with challenges.

From sleepless nights to financial crises and marital strains, Jones candidly shares the struggles that accompany the pursuit of her entrepreneurial dreams. Yet, amidst the chaos, her narrative is infused with humor and warmth, making it a delightful read.

*The Mumpreneur Diaries* serves as both a cautionary tale and an inspiration for aspiring mumpreneurs, offering valuable insights into the realities of balancing motherhood and entrepreneurship. Jones' down-to-earth approach and witty storytelling make this 'mumoir' a captivating and motivating read for anyone considering taking the leap into entrepreneurship while raising a family.

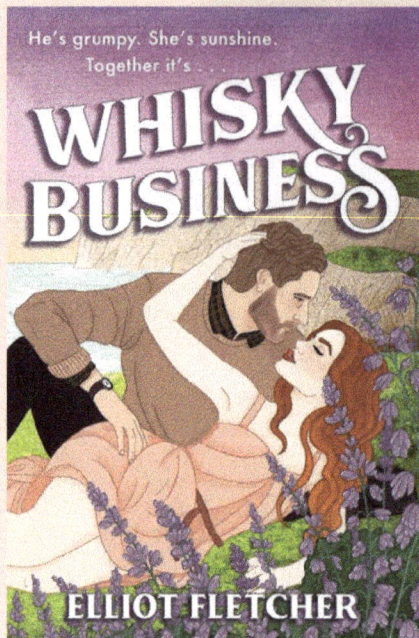

*"One flirty Hollywood actress. One grumpy Scottish islander. One magnetic connection."*

*Whisky Business* by Elliot Fletcher delivers a delightful blend of romance, humor, and whisky-soaked charm in the picturesque setting of the Isle of Skye. April Sinclair, a fallen Hollywood star, finds herself back in her Scottish hometown, determined to revive her family's whisky distillery. Little does she expect to clash with the ruggedly handsome and irritable master distiller, Malcolm Macabe.

Fletcher crafts a compelling enemies-to-lovers narrative, weaving together April and Mal's fiery chemistry with the backdrop of whisky-making traditions. Mal's gruff demeanor and April's glamorous persona create a dynamic tension that keeps the pages turning.

The Isle of Skye provides a stunning backdrop for the story, immersing readers in its rugged beauty and atmospheric charm. Fletcher's vivid descriptions bring the setting to life, evoking a sense of place that adds depth to the narrative.

But it's not just the setting that shines in "Whisky Business." The steamy romance between April and Mal adds a sizzling tension to the story, keeping readers hooked until the very end.

*Whisky Business* is a captivating romcom that balances humor, heart, and heat in equal measure. Fletcher's witty prose and irresistible characters make this a must-read for fans of enemies-to-lovers romance.

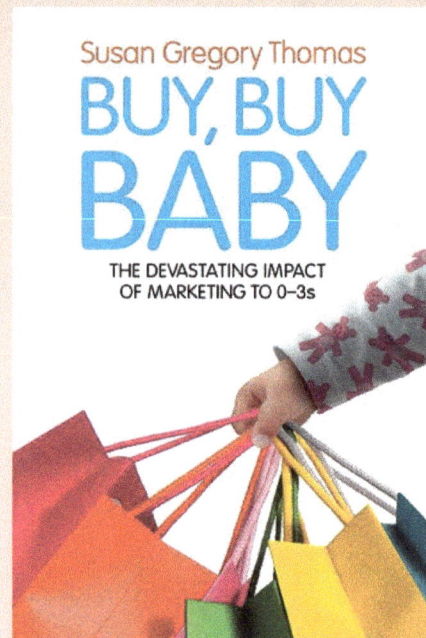

*"The book captivates with its blend of romance and intrigue, showcasing Herkness's masterful storytelling prowess. A must-read!"*

*Buy Buy Baby* by Susan Gregory Thomas offers a compelling exposé on the insidious tactics employed by multinational corporations to target infants and toddlers as consumers. Drawing parallels to seminal works like "No Logo" and "Fast Food Nation," Thomas unveils the unsettling reality of how big business manipulates parental anxieties and exploits child development research to peddle products to the youngest demographic.

With meticulous research, Thomas delves into the marketing strategies that saturate the market with seemingly educational toys and media, masking profit-driven agendas. She adeptly navigates through the landscape of brands like Disney, McDonald's, and Barbie, revealing their pervasive influence on young minds.

As a parent and seasoned journalist, Thomas brings a unique perspective to the discussion, underscoring the detrimental effects of consumerism on early childhood development. Her insights shed light on the alarming rise of anxiety and hyper-competitiveness among children, echoing the concerns of many contemporary parents.

*Buy Buy Baby* is not just a critique of corporate practices; it's a call to action against the commodification of childhood. Thomas's work serves as a timely reminder of the ethical implications of marketing to vulnerable demographics and underscores the urgent need for conscientious consumption.

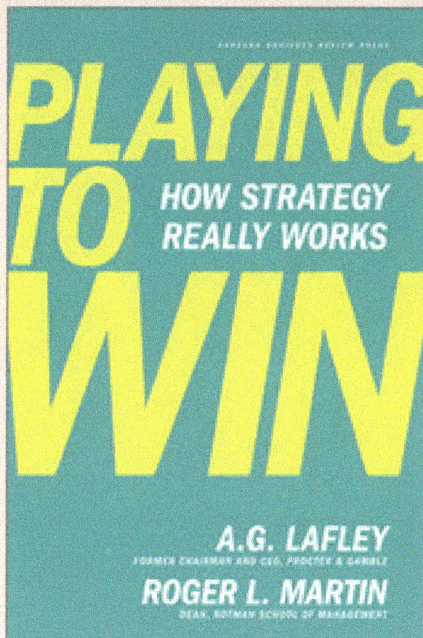

## PLAYING TO WIN
### by A.G. Lafley and Roger Martin

*"Essential playbook for strategic success. Lafley and Martin offer practical wisdom that transforms businesses. A must-read for aspiring leaders."*

*Playing to Win: How Strategy Really Works* by A.G. Lafley and Roger Martin is a must-read for anyone looking to understand the essence of successful business strategy. Drawing from his extensive experience as CEO of Procter & Gamble, Lafley, along with strategic adviser Roger Martin, provides a comprehensive guidebook for navigating the complexities of modern business.

Through compelling narratives and insightful analysis, Lafley and Martin unveil the strategic approach that propelled P&G to unprecedented success during Lafley's tenure. By focusing on essential elements such as where to play and how to win, the authors demonstrate how leaders can align everyday actions with overarching strategic goals to achieve remarkable results.

The book is not merely a theoretical exposition; it is a practical playbook filled with real-world examples of how P&G transformed iconic brands like Olay, Gillette, and Swiffer into market leaders through strategic decision-making. Lafley's return to P&G underscores the enduring relevance of the strategies outlined in this book, making it essential reading for executives, entrepreneurs, and anyone seeking to gain a competitive edge in today's dynamic business landscape.

*Playing to Win* is a compelling blend of theory and practice, offering invaluable insights that will undoubtedly resonate with readers striving not just to play the game, but to emerge victorious.

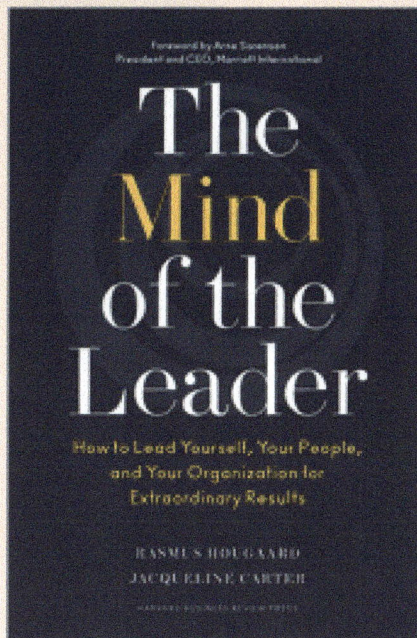

## THE MIND OF THE LEADER
### by Rasmus Hougaard and Jacqueline Carter

*"The Mind of the Leader offers a transformative approach, advocating mindfulness, selflessness, and compassion, providing actionable strategies for effective leadership.*

*The Mind of the Leader: How to Lead Yourself, Your People, and Your Organization for Extraordinary Results* by Rasmus Hougaard and Jacqueline Carter presents a compelling argument for a fundamental shift in leadership philosophy. Backed by comprehensive research and insightful interviews, the book sheds light on a pressing global issue: the disconnect between leaders and their teams.

Hougaard and Carter paint a stark picture of the current leadership landscape, where despite significant investments in development, employees feel disengaged and undervalued. Through their exploration of the basic human needs of meaning, purpose, connection, and happiness in the workplace, they pinpoint the root of this disengagement.

What sets "The Mind of the Leader" apart is its pragmatic approach to tackling the leadership crisis. By advocating for mindfulness, selflessness, and compassion as core mental qualities for effective leadership, the authors offer a refreshing perspective. Drawing on real-world examples from top organizations, they demonstrate how embracing these qualities can lead to transformative results.

This book is not just a critique of existing leadership paradigms; it's a roadmap for change. It challenges leaders to prioritize people over profits and provides actionable strategies for doing so. *The Mind of the Leader* is a must-read for anyone invested in fostering a more inclusive, compassionate, and ultimately successful organizational culture.

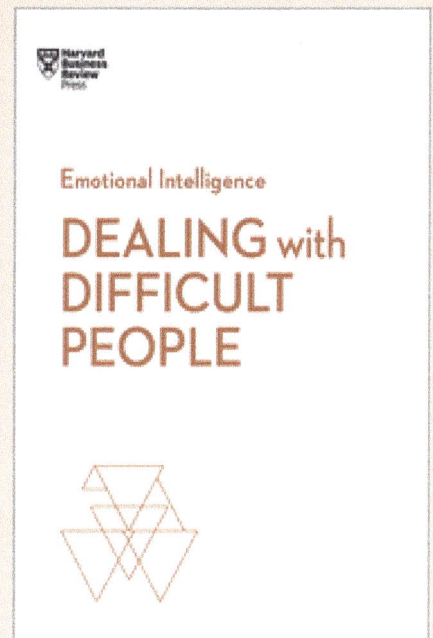

## DEALING WITH DIFFICULT PEOPLE
### by Harvard Business Review, Tony Schwartz, Mark Gerzon, Holly Weeks, Amy Gallo

*"Insightful and practical advice from expert contributors. Essential reading for mastering workplace dynamics and fostering productive relationships effectively."*

*Dealing with Difficult People* is a comprehensive guide to navigating the challenging dynamics often encountered in professional environments. Authored by a team of experts including Tony Schwartz, Mark Gerzon, Holly Weeks, and Amy Gallo, the book delves into the intricate interplay of emotions that characterize interactions with troublesome colleagues.

Central to its message is the importance of managing emotions, both one's own and those of others, in order to foster more productive relationships. Through a blend of research-backed insights and practical advice, the book equips readers with the tools to remain composed during tough conversations and to effectively address passive-aggressive behavior.

Part of the acclaimed HBR Emotional Intelligence Series, this book offers essential reading for anyone seeking to enhance their interpersonal skills in the workplace. It not only provides strategies for managing difficult individuals but also encourages self-reflection to recognize one's own contributions to workplace dynamics.

With contributions from renowned thought leaders in the field, *Dealing with Difficult People* is a valuable resource for ambitious professionals looking to cultivate empathy, resilience, and emotional intelligence in their pursuit of success. Uplifting and practical, it offers actionable insights that are indispensable for navigating the complexities of professional relationships.

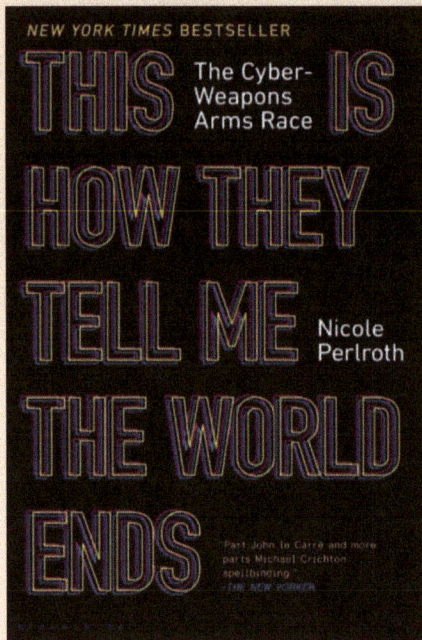

## THIS IS HOW THEY TELL ME THE WORLD ENDS

### by *Nicole Perlroth*

*"Nicole Perlroth's "This Is How They Tell Me the World Ends" is nothing short of a masterpiece in investigative journalism."*

Nicole Perlroth's *This Is How They Tell Me the World Ends* is a chilling exposé delving into the clandestine realm of cyberweapons, unearthing a world veiled in secrecy yet wielding immense power over global security. Through meticulous research and riveting storytelling, Perlroth sheds light on the elusive market of zero-day exploits, the prized tools capable of infiltrating and manipulating critical systems with unprecedented stealth.

With the United States as its focal point, Perlroth unveils the unsettling reality of how governments amassed and exploited zero-days for decades, only to lose control, thereby unleashing a perilous arms race. The narrative brims with a diverse cast, from government agents to hackers, illuminating their intricate dance within this shadowy market. Against the backdrop of escalating cyber threats, Perlroth skillfully weaves together the high-stakes drama with insightful analysis, highlighting the grave implications for global security.

*This Is How They Tell Me the World Ends* not only captivates with its thriller-like narrative but also serves as a vital wake-up call. Perlroth's blend of investigative journalism and expert commentary delivers a sobering account of the urgent need to address the escalating cyber arms race. As the world grapples with mounting cyber threats, Perlroth's work stands as a compelling testament to the imperative of vigilance and cooperation in safeguarding against digital vulnerabilities. Engrossing and enlightening, this book is an essential read for anyone concerned about the future of global security in the digital age.

## JANESVILLE

### *Amy Goldstein*

*"Service's Lines in the Sand is a poignant masterpiece, weaving raw emotion and introspection into an unforgettable journey of self-discovery."*

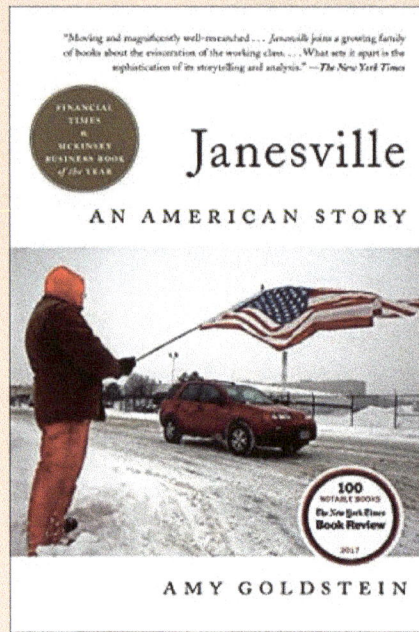

*Janesville* by Amy Goldstein is a compelling narrative that transcends the boundaries of a single town to offer a profound reflection on the broader socio-economic landscape of America. Set against the backdrop of Janesville, Wisconsin, Goldstein meticulously chronicles the aftermath of the closure of its General Motors assembly plant during the Great Recession. Unlike other accounts that focus solely on the immediate shock of job loss, Goldstein delves deep into the lives of its residents, revealing the long-term repercussions on individuals, families, and the community. Through her immersive storytelling, she portrays the resilience and resourcefulness of Janesville's inhabitants as they confront the harsh realities of economic upheaval.

One of the book's strengths lies in its diverse array of voices, capturing the perspectives of autoworkers, educators, politicians, bankers, and job re-trainers. Goldstein skillfully navigates the intersection of economics and politics, shedding light on the complex dynamics shaping contemporary America. *Janesville* is not just a local story—it is an American story that confronts readers with uncomfortable truths about the fragility of the social safety net and the daunting obstacles facing the working class. In conclusion, "Janesville" stands as a testament to the resilience of the human spirit in the face of adversity, offering a narrative of hope, perseverance, and the will to forge a brighter future against all odds.

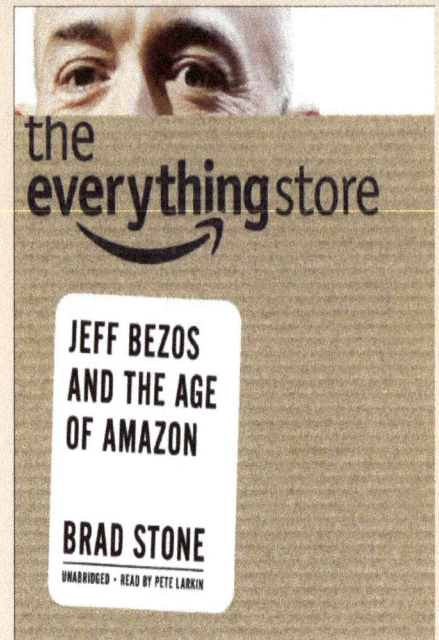

## THE EVERYTHING STORE

### by *Brad Stone*

In "The Everything Store," Brad Stone delves deep into the enigmatic world of Amazon and its pioneering founder, Jeff Bezos. From its humble beginnings as an online bookstore to its evolution into the global powerhouse it is today, Stone unveils the relentless ambition and visionary leadership that propelled Amazon to become "the everything store."

Stone paints a vivid portrait of Bezos, a man driven by an insatiable hunger for innovation and expansion. Bezos's unwavering determination to redefine retail led Amazon into uncharted territory, from the development of the Kindle to its groundbreaking ventures in cloud computing. Through meticulous research and compelling narrative, Stone illustrates how Bezos's bold decisions reshaped not only the retail landscape but also the very fabric of the internet itself.

What sets "The Everything Store" apart is its exploration of Amazon's corporate culture, characterized by an aura of secrecy and a relentless pursuit of excellence. Stone offers readers a glimpse into the inner workings of a company known for its unconventional practices and its relentless focus on customer satisfaction. By uncovering the mechanisms behind Amazon's success, Stone sheds light on the intricate balance between innovation and disruption that defines the company's ethos.

One of the most captivating aspects of Stone's narrative is his portrayal of Amazon's pivotal role in shaping the digital age. By placing one of the earliest and largest bets on the internet, Amazon not only transformed the way we shop but also paved the way for a new era of technological innovation. Through gripping storytelling and insightful analysis, Stone chronicles Amazon's journey from a fledgling startup to a titan of industry, leaving an indelible mark on the world in its wake.

In conclusion, "The Everything Store" is a captivating exploration of Amazon's rise to prominence and the visionary leadership of Jeff Bezos. Through Stone's masterful storytelling, readers are offered a front-row seat to witness the birth of a revolution in retail and technology. Whether you're an entrepreneur, a business enthusiast, or simply curious about the inner workings of one of the world's most influential companies, this book is a must-read. Stone's meticulous research and engaging prose make "The Everything Store" an essential addition to any library, offering invaluable insights into the past, present, and future of commerce in the digital age.

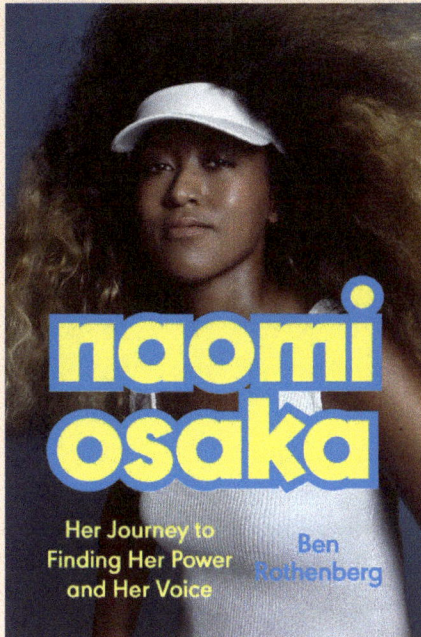

## NAOMI OSAKA
### By Ben Rothenberg

*"Rothenberg's biography of Naomi Osaka illuminates her inspiring journey, capturing her impact on tennis, social justice, and mental health."*

In *Naomi Osaka: Her Journey to Finding Her Power and Her Voice*, Ben Rothenberg delves deep into the life of the tennis sensation, uncovering the captivating narrative behind her rise to prominence. Rothenberg adeptly navigates through Osaka's meteoric ascent in the tennis world, from her headline-making victory over Serena Williams at the 2018 US Open to her subsequent triumphs on the Grand Slam stage.

What sets Rothenberg's biography apart is its focus not just on Osaka's on-court achievements but also on her off-court impact. Through meticulous research and compelling storytelling, Rothenberg sheds light on Osaka's journey as an advocate for racial justice and mental health, showcasing her as a trailblazer who transcends the boundaries of sports.

The biography also offers invaluable insights into Osaka's personal background, notably her Haitian-Japanese-American heritage and her family's unwavering support throughout her career. By unraveling the intricacies of Osaka's upbringing and her quest to navigate the complexities of fame and identity, Rothenberg paints a vivid portrait of a remarkable individual.

*Naomi Osaka* is a must-read for tennis aficionados and casual fans alike, offering a comprehensive exploration of one of the most influential figures in sports today. Rothenberg's narrative skillfully captures the essence of Osaka's resilience, determination, and unwavering commitment to making a difference both on and off the court.

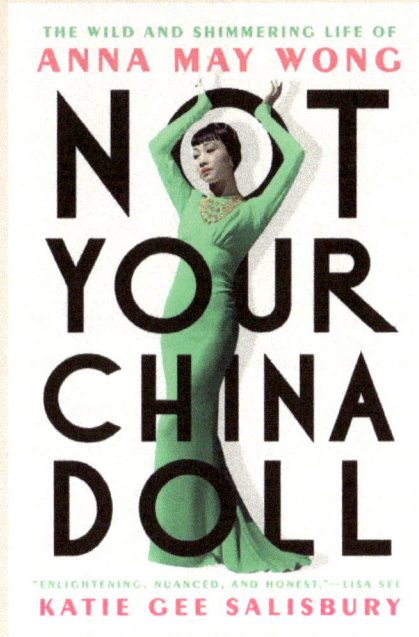

## NOT YOUR CHINA DOLL
### By Katie Gee Salisbury

*"Rothenberg's 'Not Your China Doll' captivates with vivid storytelling, celebrating Anna May Wong's groundbreaking journey in Hollywood."*

*Not Your China Doll* by Ben Rothenberg delves into the captivating journey of Anna May Wong, the trailblazing Asian American movie star of Hollywood's golden era. Rothenberg skillfully navigates Wong's ascent from humble beginnings in Los Angeles to international stardom, shedding light on her struggles against typecasting and racial stereotypes in the film industry.

Set against the glitz and glamor of 1920s Los Angeles, Rothenberg paints a vivid portrait of Wong as a legendary beauty and fashion icon who defied societal expectations. Through meticulous research and engaging prose, he chronicles her rise to fame in Douglas Fairbanks's The Thief of Bagdad and her subsequent rebellion against Hollywood's discriminatory practices.

Wong's bold decision to challenge Hollywood's racism by seeking opportunities abroad is portrayed with poignancy and admiration. Rothenberg masterfully captures the essence of Wong's audacity and resilience as she navigates through a world of capricious directors, glamorous parties, and far-flung love affairs.

*Not Your China Doll* is a compelling tribute to a pioneering artist who paved the way for future generations of Asian American actors. Rothenberg's debut book is a must-read for anyone interested in cinema history and the ongoing struggle for representation in the entertainment industry.

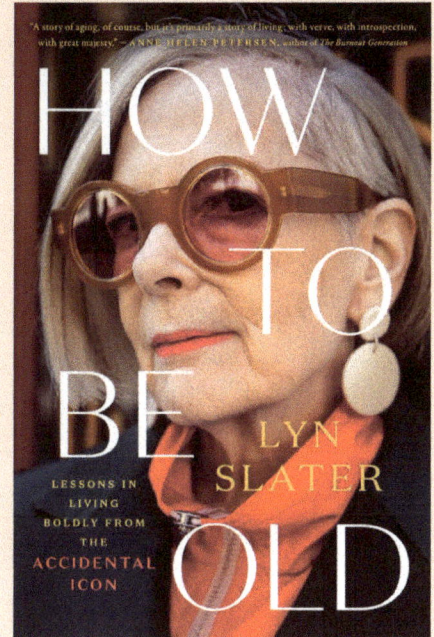

## HOW TO BE OLD
### By Lyn Slater

*"How to Be Old" by Lyn Slater empowers readers to embrace aging boldly, redefine beauty standards, and live life on their terms.*

*How to Be Old* by Lyn Slater, also known as the "Accidental Icon," is a refreshing and empowering memoir that challenges societal norms surrounding aging. Through her personal journey documented over a decade, Slater proves that age is merely a number and should not limit one's ability to live boldly and authentically.

Slater's candid storytelling and unapologetic embrace of her gray hair and wrinkles serve as an inspiration for readers of all ages. She rejects the notion of fading into the background as one grows older and instead encourages readers to redefine their perceptions of aging. Her message resonates deeply, emphasizing the importance of self-acceptance and embracing change with optimism and creativity.

With wit and wisdom, Slater demonstrates that the process of reinvention knows no bounds. She encourages readers to challenge societal standards of beauty and youth, advocating for a more inclusive and empowering definition of successful aging. Through her narrative, Slater showcases the potential for growth, connection, and creativity in every stage of life.

*How to Be Old* is not just a memoir; it's a manifesto for living life on one's own terms. Slater's fearless approach to aging serves as a beacon of hope and empowerment for readers seeking to navigate the complexities of getting older. This paradigm-shifting book is a must-read for anyone looking to embrace the fullness of life at any age.

# Empowering Entrepreneurship: The Journey of Chris Maslin

*Chris Maslin founded Go EO, empowering business transitions to employee ownership. Overcoming challenges, he streamlined services, emphasizing innovation, community impact, and financial acumen. His journey inspires collaborative empowerment in entrepreneurship.*

In the bustling world of entrepreneurship, where innovation and ambition intersect, stories of visionaries carving their path towards success often stand out. Chris Maslin, the dynamic founder of Go EO, embodies this spirit of innovation and empowerment. In an exclusive interview with Entrepreneur Prime magazine, Maslin shares his journey from a driven accountant to a pioneering advocate for employee ownership trusts.

Based in Kent, Maslin's venture into entrepreneurship was not just about creating another business; it was about revolutionizing the landscape of ownership and empowerment. Drawing from his own experience of transforming his accountancy firm into a trust, Maslin recognized the transformative potential of providing an affordable exit strategy for business owners while ensuring their teams had a stake in the company's future.

"What inspired you to start your business?" The question posed to Maslin unveils a narrative of purpose and determination. His journey was not merely about financial gain but about instilling a sense of purpose and value in every venture undertaken.

Navigating the tumultuous waters of entrepreneurship, Maslin encountered his fair share of challenges, particularly in acquiring those crucial first customers. Yet, fuelled by his unwavering belief in his vision, he overcame these obstacles, laying the foundation for his subsequent successes.

The genesis of Maslin's business ideas lies in perceiving gaps in the market and ingeniously streamlining services to offer cost-effective solutions. This approach, akin to "IKE-A-ising" services, has proven to be a game-changer, democratising access to essential business strategies.

Reflecting on his journey, Maslin dispenses invaluable advice to aspiring entrepreneurs, emphasizing the importance of innovation, adaptability, and financial acumen. His insights resonate with clarity, offering a roadmap for those embarking on their entrepreneurial odyssey.

Moreover, Maslin's ethos extends beyond business success; it encompasses a commitment to giving back to his community, evident through his charitable endeavours in Tunbridge Wells. His dedication to creating a positive impact underscores the essence of entrepreneurship as a force for good.

In a world where entrepreneurship is often synonymous with individual success, Chris Maslin stands as a beacon of collaborative empowerment. Through Go EO, he not only facilitates business transitions but also fosters a culture of shared ownership and prosperity. As entrepreneurs embark on their own quests for success, Maslin's journey serves as a testament to the transformative power of innovation, resilience, and unwavering dedication.

## What inspired you to start your business?

As an employee, I was like the stereotypical four year old. My manager would ask me to do something. I'd ask why, or query whether I could do it a different way. I'd be told to just get on with it. I've always been happy to work, but I need to understand the purpose, feel what I'm doing is worthwhile, and do it in a way I accept is sensible. I think I was destined to run my own business!

## What challenges did you find at the beginning of your journey and how did you overcome them?

Getting those first few customers! It's an obvious hurdle, but one people from the employed world may under estimate.

## How did you get the idea for your business and why did you think it would work?

The initial business was an accountancy firm. I've set up two further businesses since then (MVL Online and Go EO). Both are based on what I perceived to be a gap in the market. I've heard them referred to as "IKE-A-ising". Take what was previously a bespoke service offering, limit the choice so you can streamline things then offer at a significantly lower cost.

## How did you raise the money to start your business?

It's a myth that you need a lot of money to start a business. So many businesses these days can be started with just a PC and internet connection. I've always been frugal, so from a few years employed as an accountant, combined with my wife's salary, we had about £10k savings when I quit my employed role. That £10k was the buffer, for living costs, whilst income picked up. It initially took a lot longer than I'd hoped to get any reasonable level of income… but once I'd got over that early hurdle, things snowballed.

## What motivates you to keep going?

I'm now in the lucky situation where business success to date combined with inexpensive tastes means I already have more money than I need. I'm working because I want to, rather than because I have to. I still get motivation from a sense of achievement and doing good in the world. Also just alleviating boredom(!) I couldn't enjoy the rest of my life rotating between holidays and golf!

## What makes your business unique?

With my current business Go EO, nothing it provides is unique. Yet I still feel there's a big gap in the market that it's aiming to fill. In effect it'll be providing a basic, affordable version of many things related to Employee Ownership. We already do this for business sales to Employee Ownership Trusts. We'll soon be doing this with share option schemes.

## What advice would you give to someone who is trying to become an entrepreneur?

You don't need to invent something totally new. You do need to do something a little differently to the rest of the market. You do need to be able to sell and be reasonably good with finances.

## What are your tips for employing a team?

Start small. Perhaps start with freelancers, or a part time employee.

Don't micromanage. Firstly, it's massively de-motivating for the employee, suggesting you don't trust them. Secondly, it will limit your growth, as you checking everything will become the bottleneck. Let them know what you want them to achieve, then let them do it their way. Check in on the results and offer support.

# THE RISKS OF DIY DENTISTRY

## Why Some Things Are Best Left to Professionals

*"DIY dentistry poses risks like irreversible damage and overlooked issues. ADA warns against at-home treatments, emphasizing personalized care from dentists for safe, effective solutions and long-term oral health."*

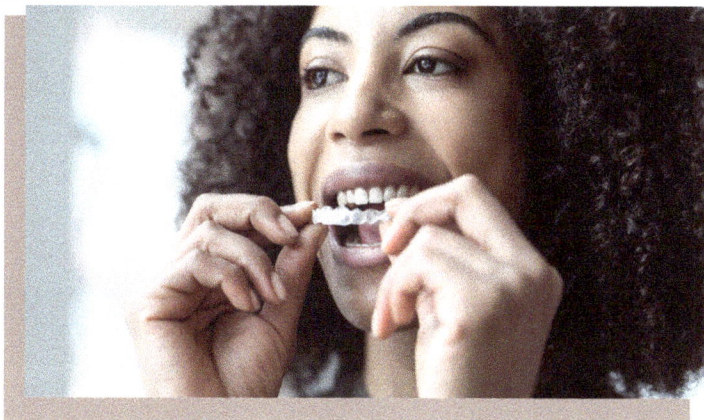

PHOTO BY NENSURIA / ISTOCK VIA GETTY IMAGES PLUS

DIY activities, like swapping a lighting fixture or painting your living room, are popular ways to accomplish your to-do list. But as anyone who has tackled too big of a project knows, some jobs are best left to the professionals. That includes your dental health.

You may have already seen DIY dentistry products, such as at-home whitening kits, mouthguards or teeth aligners. These often guarantee fast, easy ways to solve your oral health issues without the involvement of a dentist or an orthodontist (a dentist who specializes in the bite and alignment of your teeth).

"Dental products are never one-size-fits-all," said American Dental Association (ADA) president, Linda Edgar, D.D.S. "No two mouths are alike, which is why it's important to work directly with an ADA dentist or orthodontist to determine the precise care that your body needs."

Skipping the dentist chair and "fixing" your teeth at home can lead to bigger, sometimes irreversible problems. For some people with more complex dental health needs, using an at-home aligner may cause bone loss, lost teeth, receding gums, bite problems, jaw pain and other damaging and permanent issues. You might also not be aware of other dental issues that should be addressed before you start moving teeth.

"Patients are understandably drawn to these DIY treatments because they might struggle to fit a dentist appointment into their schedule or they assume at-home care will cost less," Dr. Edgar said.

*"Don't gamble with your oral health. Consult a dentist for safe, effective treatment."*

"But when these products cause major issues, patients end up spending more time and more money trying to reverse that damage. Instead, trained ADA dentists and orthodontists can talk through patients' budget concerns and offer them a wider variety of dependable, approved treatment options."

In between dental checkups, look for products with the ADA Seal of Acceptance. These have been independently evaluated by experts and recognized to be both safe and effective. When you choose one of these options, you can be assured that your care is backed by evidence-based research and generations of scientific knowledge.

Whether it's teeth grinding or a toothache, talk to your dentist before trying to solve your dental problems on your own. A dentist can help you find a personalized treatment plan that's right for you, monitor your progress and make recommendations on how to manage your oral health outside of the office.

To look for an ADA dentist in your area, visit findadentist.ada.org.

"The ADA's primary concerns with DIY dentistry are, and always have been, patient safety and quality care," Dr. Edgar said. "Our job as dentists is to put patient health first." (STATE POINT)

Triple Emmy winning keynote speaker Gaby Natale delivers an inspiring keynote at Google's Silicon Valley campus, emphasizing pioneering leadership and inclusivity to foster innovation and resilience in today's rapidly evolving world.

# Breaking Barriers
## Gaby Natale Inspires at Google with Pioneering Leadership Keynote

*Gaby Natale, a triple Emmy-winning speaker, delivered an inspiring keynote at Google, emphasizing pioneering leadership, inclusivity, and breaking barriers to foster innovation and resilience in today's rapidly changing world.*

In a landmark event that brought together innovation and inspiration, three-time Emmy Award-winning journalist and bestselling author Gaby Natale delivered a compelling keynote address at Google's Silicon Valley campus. Known for her transformative insights and pioneering leadership message, Natale captivated the audience with her vision of breaking barriers and redefining leadership in today's fast-paced world.

Natale, a trailblazer in her own right, shared her unique perspective on how leaders can cultivate a pioneering spirit to drive innovation, inclusivity, and resilience. Drawing from her extensive research and personal journey of overcoming obstacles, she emphasized the need to challenge outdated leadership models and embrace a future filled with possibilities.

"Pioneering leadership isn't just about being first. It's about redefining what's possible, embracing change, and having the courage to lead with authenticity and purpose," Natale asserted. Her message resonated deeply with Google's commitment to fostering a culture of belonging and inclusivity, aligning perfectly with the tech giant's mission to make information universally accessible and useful.

Google, a subsidiary of Alphabet Inc., continues to be a global powerhouse, shaping the lives of billions through its diverse range of products and platforms, including Search, Maps, Gmail, Android, Google Play, Google Cloud, Chrome, and YouTube. The company's dedication to innovation and inclusivity was a central theme of Natale's keynote, highlighting the importance of creating environments where everyone can thrive.

## ABOUT GABY NATALE

Gaby Natale is a force to be reckoned with. As the first Latina to win three consecutive Daytime Emmy Awards as both host and executive producer of her own show, she has consistently broken new ground. Her achievements extend beyond television; she is also the first Hispanic author published by HarperCollins' Leadership division and one of the few foreign-born writers to narrate their audiobook in English.

A sought-after motivational speaker, Natale has shared her empowering message with Fortune 500 companies, the United Nations, and through her TEDx talk, encouraging underrepresented minorities to pioneer and become what they cannot yet see in the world. Her bestselling book, "The Virtuous Circle," topped Amazon's New Releases charts in Business, Inspiration, and Self-Help categories.

Natale is the founder of AGA-NARmedia, a marketing company focused on Hispanic audiences, serving major clients like Hilton Worldwide, Sprint, AT&T, eBay, Intuit, and Amazon. With over 52 million views on YouTube and a robust social media following, her influence extends across digital platforms.

A passionate advocate for gender and diversity issues, Natale collaborates with nonprofits such as Susan G. Komen and Voto Latino. Her work has been recognized by Forbes, CNN, Buzzfeed, NBC News, Univision, and Latino Leaders magazine. She is the recipient of NALIP's Digital Trailblazer Award and a GLAAD Media Award nomination for her portrayal of Latino LGBTQ youth in media.

Natale holds a bachelor's degree in International Relations and a master's degree in Journalism from the University of San Andres. Before her television career, she taught Communication and Journalism at the University of Texas.

Gaby Natale's keynote at Google was not just a speech; it was a call to action for leaders everywhere to embrace change, foster inclusivity, and unlock their greatest potential. Her pioneering spirit continues to inspire and pave the way for future generations.

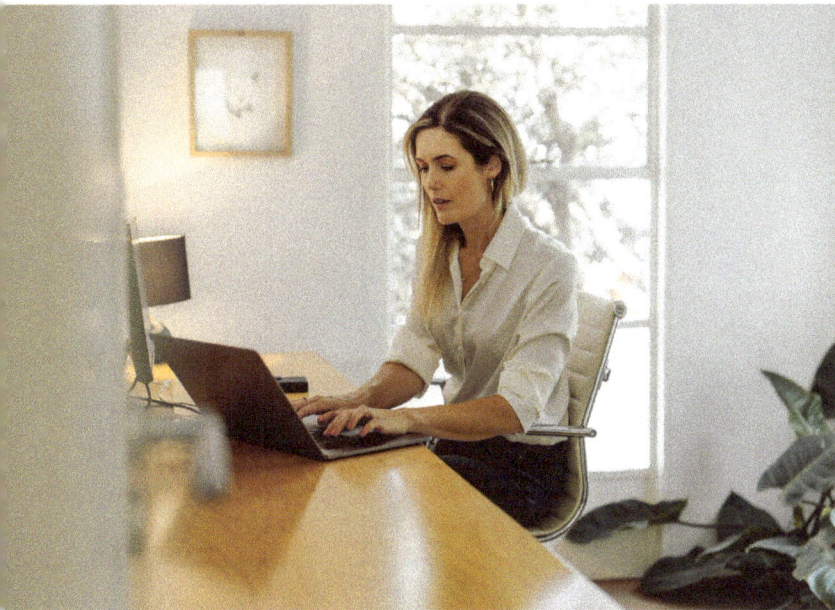

# Financial Planning: A Great Career Option for Remote Work

*Remote work is highly desired, especially for CERTIFIED FINANCIAL PLANNER® professionals, who enjoy job security, flexibility, and satisfaction, with a predicted 13% demand increase by 2032.*

If you're like most workers today, you see remote work as a major perk. In fact, a Buffer study finds that 98% of all workers have expressed the desire to work remotely, at least part of the time.

Fortunately, high-earning potential and the flexibility to work anywhere often go hand-in-hand for those on the path to becoming a CERTIFIED FINANCIAL PLANNER® professional. Here's why, and what it means for you:

**An in-demand field:** The Bureau of Labor and Statistics predicts that demand for financial planners will increase at a rate of 13% through 2032, meaning financial planners enjoy job security and plentiful career opportunities at firms of many types and sizes. And CFP® certification only makes your job more secure — 86% of consumers prefer an advisor who has completed a rigorous education program and passed a certification exam.

**Broad parameters:** CFP® professionals work in a variety of settings. Many CFP® professionals start their own business — acting as their own boss, deciding on their pay structure and working wherever they wish. Some financial firms that hire CFP® professionals also have remote options. Holistic financial planning advice can be delivered in person or virtually, allowing for a great deal of location flexibility.

**Scheduling flexibility:** Where you work is just one piece of the equation. What about when you work? It's not uncommon to have a lot of schedule flexibility as a financial planner, especially if you lead your own practice. You can design a work week that aligns with your personal life, family needs and outside pursuits.

Job satisfaction: Financial planning is a helping profession. Financial planners help their clients achieve financial goals, navigate life's challenges and even help close wealth gaps. Many CFP® professionals also serve those in need through pro bono financial planning. In addition, the flexibility of financial planning makes this one career path that provides plenty of job satisfaction. In fact, 89% of CFP® professionals are satisfied with their decision to pursue certification.

To learn more about career options with a CFP® certification, visit https://www.cfp.net.

As you embark on a financial planning career, be sure to secure credentials that will not only increase your earning potential and drive your career forward but also expand your opportunities so that you can work where and when you want. (StatePoint)

# Pioneering Strategic HR Leadership

*The Hearth Podcast's new season explores HR's evolving role as a strategic thought partner, featuring expert insights on integrating HR into business strategy and fostering innovation for organizational success.*

In an exciting development for human resources professionals and enthusiasts, The Hearth Podcast has announced the launch of its new season, focusing on the evolving role of HR as a thought partner within organizations. This season promises to delve into the transformative impact HR can have when integrated as a strategic partner in business operations.

The Hearth Podcast, known for its insightful discussions and expert interviews, aims to shed light on the dynamic nature of HR in today's rapidly changing business environment. As companies increasingly recognize the value of human capital, HR's role is shifting from traditional administrative functions to becoming a pivotal player in strategic decision-making processes.

This season will feature a series of episodes that explore various aspects of HR's evolving role. Listeners can expect to hear from industry leaders, HR experts, and thought leaders who will share their experiences and insights on how HR can drive organizational success. Topics will include the integration of HR in strategic planning, the importance of fostering a culture of innovation, and the ways in which HR can contribute to achieving business objectives.

The podcast aims to provide valuable perspectives on how HR professionals can position themselves as thought partners, capable of influencing and guiding organizational strategy. By highlighting real-world examples and best practices, The Hearth Podcast seeks to inspire HR professionals to embrace their roles as strategic partners and thought leaders.

Listeners can tune in to the new season of The Hearth Podcast on major streaming platforms. Whether you are an HR professional looking to enhance your strategic impact or a business leader seeking to understand the value of HR as a thought partner, this season promises to offer valuable insights and practical advice.

As the business landscape continues to evolve, The Hearth Podcast remains committed to exploring the critical role of HR in shaping the future of work. Don't miss out on this opportunity to gain a deeper understanding of how HR can drive innovation and success in your organization.

Photo courtsey of Fortress and Flourish

*Candice Elliott, Fractional CHRO in Santa Cruz, CA, shares her expertise in strategic HR leadership and innovation.*

### KEY TAKEAWAYS FROM THE EPISODE:

• Embracing practices like locally sourcing food and biodynamic agriculture can inspire the creation of healthier and more resilient work environments.

• Prioritizing sustainable practices can counteract the negative impacts of industrialization, benefiting both people and the environment.

• Cultivating grounding and connection in hybrid and remote work settings enhances employee well-being and fosters a supportive culture.

• Effective workload management promotes sustained productivity while ensuring employees remain balanced and energized.

• Developing a strong social infrastructure within organizations supports employees in caring for children and elders, fostering a deeper sense of connection and community.

# Carver Bancorp, Inc. Appoints Donald Felix as New President and CEO

*Carver Bancorp, Inc. appoints Donald Felix as President and CEO, effective November 1, 2024, to drive growth and innovation, reinforcing its commitment to community development and financial inclusion.*

In a significant leadership transition, Carver Bancorp, Inc. has announced the appointment of Donald Felix as its new President and Chief Executive Officer, effective November 1, 2024. This strategic move marks a new chapter for the renowned financial institution, which has been a cornerstone in community banking.

Donald Felix brings a wealth of experience and a visionary approach to his new role at Carver Bancorp. With a distinguished career in the banking sector, Felix is poised to lead the company into a new era of growth and innovation. His appointment is expected to bolster Carver's commitment to serving its community and expanding its reach in the financial industry.

Felix succeeds the outgoing CEO, who has been instrumental in steering the company through challenging times and setting a solid foundation for future success. Under Felix's leadership, Carver Bancorp aims to enhance its service offerings and strengthen its position as a leader in community banking.

The board of directors expressed their confidence in Felix's ability to drive the company forward, citing his impressive track record and dedication to fostering inclusive financial solutions. As Carver Bancorp looks to the future, stakeholders and customers alike are eager to see the positive impact of Felix's leadership.

Stay tuned as Carver Bancorp embarks on this exciting new journey under the guidance of Donald Felix, promising a future filled with innovation, growth, and community-focused initiatives.

- Carver is a historic institution founded in 1948 to help underserved communities in New York City build wealth.

- Carver continues to pay its mission forward, focusing on Minority and Women Business Enterprises and the growing middle-income neighborhoods it serves.

- Approximately $0.80 of each deposit dollar at the Bank is reinvested in the diverse communities it serves through competitively priced loan capital.

- Donald Felix is only the sixth CEO in Carver's 76-year history.

*PHOTO: Felix brings more than two decades of banking leadership to advance Carver into its next era of growth.*

*Photo courtesy of Carver Bank.*

### DONALD FELIX

*Prior to his employment with Carver, Mr. Felix served as Executive Vice President of Citizens Financial Group, Head of National Banking & Expansion from 2021 to 2023. Before that, he served as Managing Director of JPMorgan Chase, in the Consumer Bank as Head of Consumer Financial Health from 2019 to 2021. He was also the Chief of Staff in the Office of the CEO, for Chase Consumer Bank & Wealth Management, from 2016 to 2019, and before joining Chase held various senior positions domestically and abroad at Citi from 1996 to 2016.*

*He holds an MBA in Finance and Strategic Management from The Wharton School, University of Pennsylvania, and a BBA in Information Systems and Analysis from Howard University. He is a Director at the Urban League of Eastern Massachusetts.*

*A first-generation Caribbean-American, Mr. Felix was born and raised in New York City and has a deep connection and long history of civic engagement with the communities that Carver serves.*

PHOTO: *Enis Hulli, General Partner at 500 Emerging Europe, is redefining the future of innovation in the regional startup ecosystem.*

# *Pioneering Global Success from Emerging Europe*
# ENIS HULLI
## *Bridging the Gap Between Regional Talent and Global Markets*

BY ONAT ONCU

*Enis Hulli, General Partner at 500 Emerging Europe, discusses his journey, investment philosophy, and strategies for transforming regional startups into global competitors by bridging Emerging Europe with Silicon Valley.*

In the dynamic world of entrepreneurship, few figures have made as significant an impact as Enis Hulli, General Partner at 500 Emerging Europe. With a solid foundation in engineering and a deep understanding of the startup ecosystem, Enis has been instrumental in unlocking the global potential of regional startups. His journey from establishing firstseed, an early-stage investment network, to becoming a key player at 500 Emerging Europe highlights his unwavering dedication to fostering innovation and growth. Enis's mission goes beyond mere investment; he is committed to transforming Emerging Europe into a hub of global entrepreneurial success.

Enis Hulli's achievements in the venture capital arena are truly commendable. His strate-

gic insights and commitment to excellence have elevated 500 Emerging Europe to a prominent position within the global startup community. By creating a vital link between Emerging Europe and Silicon Valley, Enis has empowered numerous entrepreneurs to expand their reach and realize their global ambitions. His efforts have not only driven the success of individual startups but have also redefined the venture capital landscape in the region. As you explore this engaging interview, you'll gain a deeper understanding of the vision and expertise that make Enis Hulli a pioneering force in entrepreneurship.

**Can you share a bit about your career journey and what led you to become a General Partner at 500 Emerging Europe?**

Bored during my college years,

I found myself wondering about different business ideas and eventually co-founded a start-up while I was only 20. Looking back, I definitely was not cut out for it and the company eventually failed. I tried my luck joining Rocket Internet for a brief timeframe but they soon decided to shut down that venture entirely. This experience pushed me in a more risk-averse direction, as I started to make money installing HVAC systems for a few years – leveraging my Civil Engineering degree only to feel unfulfilled and hungry to be able to spend my time at a job where I can learn and grow more.

This is the core reason why I delved into books and podcasts about entrepreneurship and started angel investing after I made some money. It eventually turned into an angel network and around the same time I met with 500 Startups.

The opportunity to be able to take a stab at building my own venture capital fund was just too good to refuse so I slowly winded down the HVAC operations and jumped ship to build my own fund as a 25-year old.

### What were some of the biggest challenges you faced when you first entered the venture capital industry, and how did you overcome them?

As a 25-year-old with no substantial track record and a failed start-up experience, it was challenging to gain people's trust.

*Enis Hulli is a visionary leader, transforming Emerging Europe's startup ecosystem with strategic insight and unwavering dedication to innovation.*

It took me two years to gather a few supporters to help build an angel network. Angel networks are different from VC funds since their investors do have a say in how the money is allocated. For a young person with a contrarian thesis and strong self-belief, the most significant hurdle is earning enough trust initially to build upon. The initial believers are crucial as they pave the way to success. Building trust, demonstrating strong commitment, and showing momentum are critical to gaining enough support to overcome that first major hurdle.

### Can you elaborate on your investment philosophy and the criteria you look for when evaluating potential start-ups?

Emerging Europe is distinct from other emerging markets, or even European funds, in that all unicorns are globally oriented companies. The successful companies in Emerging Europe generate revenues from international markets, raise capital from international VCs, and plan for exits or IPOs in international markets. The thesis revolves around betting on local talent potential while hedging against other market factors, from early customers to scaling revenue to fundraising. This necessitates a different investment thesis than a typical VC, who is making a significant bet within their geography across multiple dimensions.

Our thesis on finding global success stories from Emerging Europe turns traditional scouting on its head. Instead of simply seeking the best entrepreneurs in the region, we look for the best entrepreneurs globally who are from Emerging Europe and are inclined to build their technology teams here. The number of opportunities is much more limited when you aim for all your companies to compete globally, but the potential scale of these opportunities is much higher. Given this finite nature of opportunities, our thesis revolves around maximizing access to the best deals.

### What are some unique opportunities and challenges you see in the start-up ecosystem of Emerging Europe?

To hedge against the liquidity crunch in the region, we aim to find entrepreneurs with a global focus who can secure their next round of financing from international investors. This creates a financing value chain drift, where a start-up initially engaging with VCs from Emerging Europe can eventually attract Silicon Valley investors. Historical success stories from the region validate this thesis, as all unicorns have raised the majority of their funding from US investors. Similarly, our portfolio has raised over $1 billion, predominantly from the US.

This presents a significant challenge for founders, who sometimes have to relocate prematurely at the pre-seed stage to build a network in the Bay Area. Starting with the right early customers and design partners, they quickly move into fundraising mode, aiming to onboard US VCs. While this strategy has obvious long-term benefits, it also involves compromises in the short term concerning team culture, product development speed, and foregoing easily attainable customers in the region.

The biggest opportunity lies in the exceptional talent available in Emerging Europe. We anchor ourselves to this belief and invest in founders who are looking to capitalize on that.

### How do you see 500 Emerging Europe contributing to the broader start-up ecosystem in the region?

We position ourselves as a bridge between Emerging Europe and Silicon Valley. This is crucial because start-ups in Emerging Europe strive to emulate Silicon Valley despite being away. The increase in the number of funds with a similar thesis to ours following our success is crucial for the region. 70% of all founders we backed are in Silicon Valley, having moved either before or shortly after our investment.

Strengthening this bridge can first create multiple ecosystems in Emerging Europe that resemble those of Israel, and eventually even position Emerging Europe as a true competitor to Silicon Valley. This approach leverages the region's advantages while fully hedging against its disadvantages.

### What advice would you give to entrepreneurs who are looking to secure funding and grow their start-ups?

Founders often make many unconscious decisions, especially at the beginning, and choosing which region to focus on is one of these. Concentrating on customers from your first or second-degree connections might position you as a regional start-up, which would later limit your fundraising options.

Fundraising is a proximity game, especially at the early stages, and a local or regional positioning would drastically reduce the pool of potential investors. We back founders who aim to position themselves and their start-ups on a global scale, opening the door to attracting international funds. This strategy increases their flexibility to fundraise and maximizes their upside potential.

# Why Financial Planning Is a Great Career Option for Women

*Financial planning is an increasingly popular and lucrative career for women, offering high salaries, work-life balance, personal fulfillment, and strong support networks, including initiatives, scholarships, and mentorships from the CFP Board.*

Financial planning was once thought of as a male-dominated industry, but that's quickly changing. The number of women getting their CERTIFIED FINANCIAL PLANNER™ certification is growing year over year — and for good reason: The benefits of entering this field as a woman are numerous. Below are a few to consider.

• It's lucrative. Financial planners are in high demand and are well-compensated for their expertise. A financial advisor can pull in a generous salary right out of the gate, and earning the right credentials can boost compensation significantly. The median income for those with CFP® certification and less than 5 years of experience is $100,000 — and that median figure grows to $206,000 with 10 or more years of experience. In general, financial advisors with CFP® certification earn 12% more than those without.

• Being a CFP® professional offers good work-life balance. With the potential to work remotely and create one's own schedule, financial planning is a career path well-suited to those looking for flexibility and a desirable work-life balance.

• Financial planning can be personally fulfilling. Providing competent, ethical financial advice that helps others achieve their life goals — from sending their children to college to securing a comfortable retirement — can be extremely gratifying.

Research also finds that female CFP® professionals have a unique dedication to providing holistic financial planning. Working as a financial planner provides opportunities to uplift and empower other women, as well as members of groups historically given fewer opportunities to accumulate wealth.

• Women who aspire to become CFP® professionals will find support in many places. CFP Board, for example, has implemented initiatives to recruit women and advance their careers.

Some firms subsidize the cost of CFP® certification and give employees time away from work to study for the CFP® exam. Additionally, women's networks and business councils can help build leadership skills and professional confidence, and many firms are even paying their employees' membership fees.

CFP Board also administers scholarships for individuals underrepresented in the field, along with a mentoring program.

To learn more and get started today on your path to becoming a CFP® professional, visit getCFPcertified.org.

With demand for personal financial advisors expected to grow significantly in the coming years, and the industry making way for more women professionals, it's worth exploring this rewarding career path.

PHOTO SOURCE: monkeybusinessimages / iStock via Getty Images Plus (StatePoint)

# From Courtroom Advocate to Career Coach
# The Inspiring Journey of Cordell Parvin

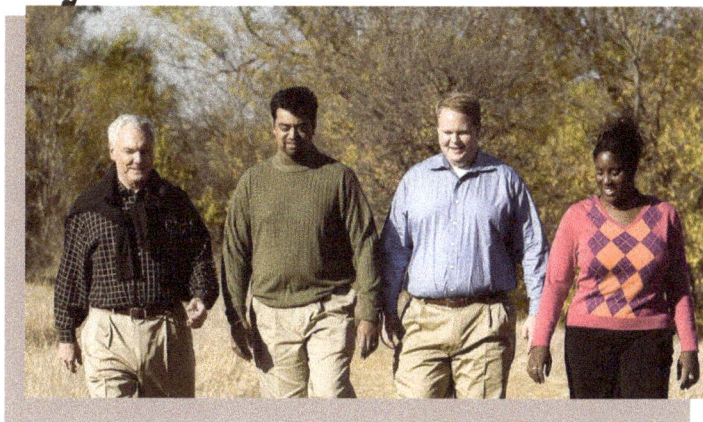

*Cordell Parvin transitioned from a successful construction lawyer to a renowned legal coach, inspiring over a thousand lawyers with his practical, storytelling approach to career development and emphasis on personal fulfillment.*

*Cordell Parvin, a trailblazing legal coach, shares his journey from practicing law to inspiring the next generation of lawyers.*

In the high-pressure and demanding realm of law, transitioning from a courtroom advocate to a career coach might appear to be an unusual path. However, for Cordell Parvin, this change has not only reshaped his own career but also inspired and guided over a thousand lawyers throughout the United States and Canada. Parvin's journey from practicing construction law to becoming a celebrated legal coach highlights the significant role of mentorship and personal satisfaction in achieving professional success.

### A Legal Career Built on Excellence

Cordell Parvin has become a prominent figure in career development within the legal field, particularly in client acquisition and professional growth for attorneys. With an impressive 38-year career in construction law, Parvin has represented some of the nation's leading contractors. Yet, it was his experience coaching new partners within his law firm that sparked a deeper passion.

In 2004, despite experiencing his most successful professional year, Parvin found greater satisfaction in assisting young lawyers with their career paths. This realization prompted him to leave his practice and fully commit to coaching lawyers. His transition from a high-earning attorney to a full-time coach marks a significant career shift motivated by a desire to make a more meaningful impact on the legal profession.

### Practical Coaching Strategies

Parvin's coaching approach is both practical and holistic, concentrating on goal setting, time management, and balancing professional duties with personal life. His strategies are informed by his extensive experience and his roles as a speaker, writer, and blogger on career and client development. Through his engaging presentations at law firms and bar associations, Parvin has established himself as a thought leader in the legal industry.

Since beginning his coaching career in 2005, Parvin has worked with lawyers from various backgrounds, offering invaluable insights into the challenges they encounter. He advocates for a structured approach to professional growth, emphasizing the importance of investing time in both career development and personal well-being. This dual focus is crucial for achieving long-term success and fulfillment in the legal profession.

### Engaging Young Lawyers Through Storytelling

Parvin's books, such as "Say Ciao to Chow Mein: Conquering Career Burnout" and "Rising Star," employ a storytelling approach inspired by Ken Blanchard's business parables. These narratives provide serious career advice in a relatable and engaging way, addressing issues like career burnout and the need for a balanced life. By sharing personal anecdotes and practical solu-

*Cordell Parvin is a visionary mentor whose transformative coaching empowers lawyers to achieve professional success and personal fulfillment.*

tions, Parvin offers young lawyers a roadmap for navigating the complexities of their careers while maintaining their well-being.

### Fostering a Collaborative Culture

One of the main challenges in the legal profession is shifting from a competitive mindset to a collaborative one. Parvin stresses the importance of fostering a collaborative culture within law firms, which can be achieved by hiring lawyers with strong interpersonal skills, rewarding teamwork, and prioritizing the development of junior lawyers. This approach not only enhances team dynamics but also creates a more supportive and productive work environment.

### Essential Advice for Aspiring Rainmakers

For young lawyers aiming to become successful rainmakers, Parvin's most vital piece of advice is to identify a compelling "why" behind their ambitions. This motivational cornerstone drives the creation of comprehensive plans, which span various timeframes and instill the commitment and discipline required to follow through. By maintaining a clear focus on their goals and understanding their underlying motivations, young lawyers can navigate their careers with greater purpose and determination.

Cordell Parvin's shift from practicing law to coaching has profoundly impacted the careers of countless lawyers. His practical, storytelling approach to career development, combined with his emphasis on personal fulfillment and collaborative culture, provides invaluable guidance to young lawyers. Parvin's journey serves as an inspiring testament to the power of mentorship and the importance of pursuing a career that aligns with one's passions and values.

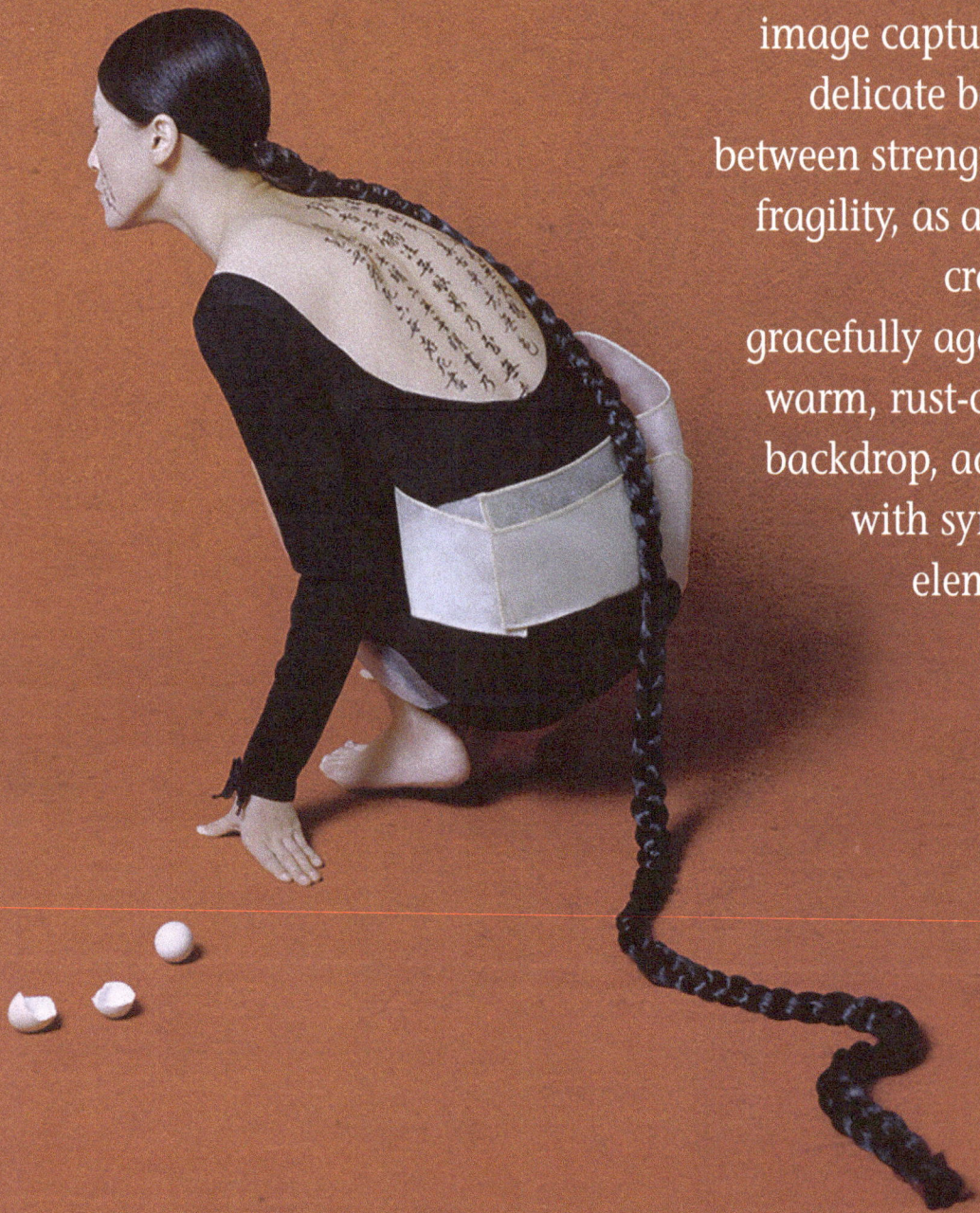

"Vulnerability, 2020: A striking composition of contrasts, this image captures the delicate balance between strength and fragility, as a figure crouches gracefully against a warm, rust-colored backdrop, adorned with symbolic elements."

## *Redefining Art and Identity*

# HAN YANG

## Discover how Han Yang blends ancient philosophies with modern technology to redefine femininity and identity

as told to Archie Preston

*Han Yang explores metaphysical nothingness and posthumanism, blending ancient and modern elements to challenge traditional gender narratives and redefine identity through her innovative art and photography.*

Han Yang, a visionary artist and fine art photographer, graces the cover of WOWwART magazine this month, bringing with her a profound exploration of art that challenges the very fabric of traditional aesthetics. Her work is a testament to the power of art to transcend boundaries and redefine norms, as she delves into the metaphysical realm of nothingness—a concept that has not only fueled her intellectual curiosity but also formed the foundation of her groundbreaking dissertations.

Han Yang's artistic journey is a harmonious blend of empirical life experiences and the timeless principles of Buddhist philosophy, expressed through a diverse array of multimedia forms. Her unique ability to visually articulate metaphysical nothingness is a hallmark of her innovative spirit, echoing the essence of ancient Zen paintings while simultaneously pushing the envelope of contemporary art.

In her photography, Han Yang masterfully intertwines themes of femininity, the human body, and technology with oriental metaphors, challenging and expanding traditional gender narratives. By integrating elements of Chinese culture with futuristic imagery, she reimagines femininity as powerful and autonomous, creating a visual dialogue that transcends cultural boundaries and redefines identity in a modern context.

Her research on posthumanism further enriches her artistic practice, allowing her to explore identity and gender through a nonhuman lens. By merging human and mechanical elements, Han Yang dissolves conventional boundaries, promoting a vision of identity that is fluid, interconnected, and liberated from traditional constraints.

Han Yang's creative process is a journey into the psychological depths of her subjects, capturing their inner worlds with a delicate balance of abstract and surreal elements. Her work navigates the intersection of commercial fashion photography and personal conceptual exploration, seamlessly blending artistic expression with market demands.

Recognized with prestigious accolades such as the SONY Young Photographer Award and the World's Top 10 Women Photographers Contest, Han Yang's career is a testament to her relentless pursuit of innovation and boundary-pushing artistry. As she continues her PhD at King's College London, her academic research and visual art practice intertwine, drawing inspiration from posthumanist and gender studies to create visual narratives that challenge and inspire.

Han Yang's work is not just art; it is a profound exploration of identity, technology, and the human condition, inviting us all to see the world through a lens of infinite possibilities.

**Your work often intertwines themes of femininity, the human body, and technology with oriental metaphors. How do you use these metaphors to challenge or enhance traditional**

**Continued** *on page 56* ➡

**Continued** *from page 55*

PAPAVER ROSES

*A whimsical dreamscape unfolds as a figure in a fluffy pink garment interacts with oversized flowers, creating an ethereal atmosphere that blurs the line between fashion and nature.*

*INVISIBLE*, 2020

*An evocative exploration of presence and absence, 'Invisible, 2020' captures the essence of what is seen and unseen, inviting viewers to ponder the hidden layers of reality.*

**narratives of gender in your photography?**

In my photography, I use oriental metaphors to challenge and expand traditional gender narratives by incorporating elements of Chinese culture into contemporary representations of femininity. I often draw on cultural symbols like ancient Chinese script, mythical creatures, and traditional garments, which embody strength, transformation, and resilience. These symbols serve as a foundation for reinterpreting femininity in a modern context.

By combining these symbols with futuristic and technological imagery, I aim to portray women as powerful and autonomous, moving away from conventional passive depictions. Technology, in my work, symbolizes evolution—indicating that gender and identity are not static, but rather fluid and ever-changing. The juxtaposition of ancient and modern elements creates a visual conversation that not only transcends cultural boundaries but also redefines femininity in a way that harmonizes tradition with progress.

**You're currently conducting research on posthumanism, particularly exploring gender through a nonhuman perspective in photography. How does this research inform your artistic practice, and how do you envision posthuman concepts reshaping our understanding of identity and gender in art?**

My research on posthumanism informs my artistic practice by allowing me to challenge conventional notions of identity and gender. Posthumanism extends the concept of the "self" beyond human limitations, embracing the influence of technology, artificial intelligence, and the environment on identity formation. In my photography, I often merge human bodies with mechanical or abstract elements, dissolving the boundaries of gender and biological traits. This exploration of nonhuman perspectives highlights gender as fluid and evolving, rather than binary or fixed. I envision posthuman concepts reshaping art by promoting identities that are hybrid, interconnected, and no longer defined by traditional physical or social constraints, allowing for more inclusive and expansive representations of the self.

*Han Yang is a visionary artist whose work transcends boundaries, redefining identity and challenging traditional narratives with profound innovation.*

**Continued** *on page 57*

**Continued** *from page 56*

**Your photography combines abstract and surreal elements with rich, delicate emotions. Can you walk us through your creative process and how you capture the psychological depth and inner world of the characters you portray?**

My creative process begins with understanding the emotional core of the concept or subject I'm working with. I spend time reflecting on the psychological nuances I want to evoke, whether it's vulnerability, strength, or transformation. From there, I incorporate abstract and surreal elements to create a visual language that mirrors these emotions without being bound by realism. I often use lighting, color, and unconventional angles to suggest an altered or dream-like reality, allowing the viewer to step into the internal world of the character. During the shoot, I work closely with the model, encouraging them to channel specific emotions, which helps bring out a raw, authentic expression. The delicate balance between surreal imagery and emotional depth is where I believe the psychological richness of my work emerges.

**As both an artist and a fine art photographer, how do you navigate the balance between fashion photography's commercial aspects and your more personal, conceptual explorations of gender and the human body?**

Navigating between the commercial nature of fashion photography and my personal conceptual work requires a constant balancing act. In fashion photography, the visual language often needs to align with brand identity and market trends, which can sometimes feel limiting.

However, I see this as an opportunity to bring my own voice into commercial projects by subtly weaving in themes of gender fluidity and the human body's complexities. When working on personal projects, I have the freedom to fully explore these concepts without constraints, diving deeper into abstract interpretations of identity and embodiment. I strive to find intersections where the artistic and commercial worlds can coexist, creating images that not only fulfil commercial needs but also provoke thought and emotion, allowing both worlds to inform and enrich each other.

**You've been recognized with prestigious awards like the SONY Young Photographer Award and the World's Top 10 Women Photographers Contest. How have these accolades influenced your career, and what role do you see awards playing in the development of your artistic voice?**

Receiving awards such as the SONY Young Photographer Award and recognition in the World's Top 10 Women Photographers Contest has greatly influenced my exploration of gender, identity, creativity, and technology. These accolades have given me the platform to delve deeper into these themes, allowing me to continue challenging traditional narratives around gender and identity through my work. They have affirmed my artistic direction and opened new pathways for creative collaborations where I can further merge technology with the human form. While awards are not the only validation, they play an important role in providing the space and recognition to push boundaries and experiment more freely, encouraging me to expand my exploration of posthumanism, fluidity, and innovation in both photography and art.

**As you pursue your PhD at King's College London, how do you integrate your academic research with your visual art practice? Are there any particular philosophical or theoretical concepts that have recently inspired your work?**

My PhD research has deeply informed and enriched my visual art practice. I explore the intersections of posthumanism, gender studies, and identity, drawing heavily from theoretical frameworks that challenge human-centric perspectives. Concepts such as Donna Haraway's cyborg theory and Rosi Braidotti's posthuman subjectivity have particularly inspired me to think beyond traditional representations of the body. These ideas resonate in my photography, where I often merge organic and mechanical elements to represent fluidity in identity and gender. The academic environment allows me to critically engage with these philosophical discourses and translate them into visual narratives. My research also helps me push the boundaries of how technology, the human form, and identity interact, making both my scholarly and artistic work extensions of each other.

> J"In my photography, I use oriental metaphors to challenge and expand traditional gender narratives."
> – Yang

# The Birth of Metaphorical Realism

## Vladimir Kush Redefines Surrealism with Metaphorical Realism, Blending Imagination and Nature in a Visionary Artistic Journey

Vladimir Kush is a renowned contemporary artist and the founder of "Metaphorical Realism," a unique artistic style that blends realism with metaphorical imagination. His works, displayed in galleries worldwide and in his own "Kush Fine Art" galleries, invite viewers to explore hidden connections between seemingly unrelated elements, offering a fresh perspective on the world.

Kush describes Metaphorical Realism as the art of discovering hidden likenesses between objects and connecting them in unexpected yet harmonious ways. Unlike traditional surrealism, which often distorts reality, his style emphasizes the internal similarities between realistic objects, creating a romantic and imaginative view of the world. For Kush, the goal is to reflect life through metaphor, finding parallels for every aspect of existence.

Metaphor, for Kush, is more than a linguistic tool—it is a way of understanding and communicating. Through metaphor, he stimulates the subconscious, awakening the viewer's imagination. He likens this process to Plato's concept of the "cave," where human souls retain core ideas of the world. Kush's art serves as a catalyst for this subconscious recollection, allowing viewers to see the familiar in a new light. "Imagination is more important than knowledge," he emphasizes, as imagination creates connections between seemingly unrelated elements.

Kush's journey from a struggling artist to an internationally acclaimed visionary is a story of perseverance. Growing up in Moscow, he was deeply influenced by classical art, literature, and the cultural values of his family. His father, a mathematician and poet, played a pivotal role in shaping his artistic sensibilities. In 1990, Kush made the bold decision to stay in the United Sta-

tes, embarking on a challenging path of self-discovery. From drawing portraits on the beaches of Santa Monica to establishing his own galleries, Kush's journey is a testament to his relentless pursuit of his vision.

The 1990s were a formative period for Kush, marked by relentless effort and the search for his unique style. By 1998, his hard work bore fruit, and he emerged as the founder of Metaphorical Realism. Iconic works like *Wind*, *Fauna in La Mancha*, *Bound for Distant Shores*, and *Music of the Woods* became defining examples of his method, laying the foundation for his artistic legacy.

Kush's creativity extends beyond painting. He has ventured into sculpture, jewelry, and even interactive apps for children, translating his artistic concepts across various mediums. "Sculptures and jewelry allow me to add another dimension to my ideas," he explains. This versatility demonstrates the universality of metaphor, proving that it can exist not only in words and paintings but also in three-dimensional forms.

While Kush cites Salvador Dali as an influence, his artistic journey was shaped by a diverse range of inspirations. His father, despite being a mathematician, was his first teacher, nurturing his love for art from an early age. Kush's artistic evolution began with Renaissance art, transitioned through Impressionism, and eventually found its voice in Surrealism. However, it was the French artist Claude Verlinde who had the greatest impact on his work.

Kush's approach to Surrealism diverges from the darker tones of Dali's era, which were shaped by war and crisis. Instead, Kush introduces a fresh, positive perspective, harmonizing his art with nature and celebrating the beauty of the world. "For the first time in art history, I have introduced a positive side of Surrealism," he says, highlighting the originality of his vision.

Kush's art has been showcased in prestigious galleries and exhibitions worldwide, from South Korea to Russia and the United States. Despite his international acclaim, Kush believes that inspiration comes from within. "If there is inner emptiness, the whole world cannot fill it," he asserts. His art transcends cultural boundaries, inviting viewers from all walks of life to see the world through the mirror of metaphor.

Vladimir Kush's contributions to contemporary art are profound and enduring. As the pioneer of Metaphorical Realism, he has redefined the way we perceive and connect with the world. His art, rich in imagination and cultural depth, serves as a bridge between the material and the metaphorical, the real and the surreal. Through his paintings, sculptures, and other creative endeavors, Kush continues to inspire audiences worldwide, reminding us of the beauty and interconnectedness of life.

*Vladimir Kush is a masterful artist whose visionary works redefine surrealism, inspiring awe with their depth, imagination, and beauty.*

" *Imagination is more important than knowledge."*

## Vladimir Kush

# Art as a Bridge Between Personal and Public Narratives

*Danica Dakić discusses how the Bosnian War influenced her art, exploring themes of identity, collectivity, and the tension between personal and public narratives through innovative media.*

Danica Dakić, a visionary artist whose work has been profoundly shaped by her experiences during the Bosnian War and the siege of Sarajevo, continues to captivate audiences with her exploration of identity, collectivity, and the interplay between personal and public narratives. An interview conducted with the artist for Mosaic Digest delves into the transformative impact of these experiences on her artistic vision and practice.

The war in Bosnia and the subsequent isolation from her homeland marked a pivotal shift in Dakić's artistic journey. During this period, she grappled with the meaning and function of art, leading her to explore new themes, media, and methods. Her installation "Blaues Auge" (1996) exemplifies this shift, addressing the disconnection between personal experience and media narratives. By collaging thousands of newspaper photos and headlines on transparent foil, Dakić created a powerful visual barrier that symbolized the opacity of media representations during times of conflict. This work, and others like it, reflect her ongoing artistic engagement with the tension between personal and public narratives.

Dakić's video installation "Grand Organ" (2010), commissioned for the Touched exhibition at St. George's Hall in Liverpool, further exemplifies her innovative approach to art. Inspired by the hall's majestic organ and neoclassical architecture, the installation explores themes of justice, performance, and music. By transforming the boys' choir into an organ with human pipe voices, composer Bojan Vuletić's sound design highlights the interplay between the legal system and spectacle. The involvement of local choirs, including the Liverpool Signing Choir and the "Sparrows" of Sparrow Hall, underscores Dakić's focus on polyphony and childhood, creating a narrative that examines power dynamics and community.

Throughout her career, Dakić has experimented with various mediums, from painting to video, sound, and text. Her choice of medium is driven by the narrative or message she wishes to convey, with each medium offering a unique way to experience her images. As an "image maker," Dakić believes in the power of images to communicate complex ideas and emotions that transcend traditional media boundaries.

Dakić's work is deeply informed by historical and social contexts, particularly in relation to identity and collectivity. While her personal experiences of war and displacement influence her exploration of these themes, her art speaks to universal experiences of mobility, migration, and living in multiple languages and cultures. Her work invites viewers to reflect on the perception of the global present and the role of the individual within larger societal structures.

The tension between individuality and collectivity is a recurring theme in Dakić's art, as seen in the allegorical references to music and law in "Grand Organ." She explores this tension on visual, acoustic, performative, and emotional levels, offering a nuanced perspective on the individual's place within society. Her art challenges viewers to consider the complexities of identity and the interconnectedness of personal and collective experiences.

Danica Dakić's artistic journey is a testament to her resilience and creativity in the face of adversity. Her work continues to inspire and provoke thought, offering a powerful commentary on the human condition and the ever-evolving narratives that shape our world. Through her innovative use of media and exploration of profound themes, Dakić has established herself as a leading voice in contemporary art, captivating audiences with her ability to transform personal experiences into universal narratives.

> **Dakić's experiences during the Bosnian War reshaped her artistic vision, leading to new themes and media explorations.**

Danica Dakić is a visionary artist whose profound insights and creativity transform personal experiences into universal narratives.

" *"The war had a strong influence on my life and my art."*

# Danica Dakić

# The Art of Vibrant Connection

*Gary Petersen explores his journey from Staten Island to international acclaim, reflecting on how residencies, awards, and solo shows have shaped his bold, vibrant approach to abstraction and his evolving color palette.*

# GARY PETERSEN

## An inside look at Petersen's creative process and inspirations

Editor's Desk

**"**The luxury of time at both residencies allowed me to explore new avenues in my work, free from the usual day-to-day distractions"

Gary Petersen's work radiates an extraordinary sense of colour, shape, and rhythm, breathing life into geometric abstraction with a style that is both playful and profound. Over the years, he has established a unique visual language, characterized by bold compositions and vibrant palettes that defy the confines of the canvas, inviting viewers to delve into layered meanings and emotional resonances. His ability to balance precision with spontaneity results in paintings that seem to vibrate with movement, a testament to his mastery of form and hue. Petersen's work not only captures the eye but also elicits an immersive experience—one that has earned him a well-deserved place in prestigious collections and institutions worldwide, including the Jewish Museum and the Dallas Museum of Art. From his studios in Brooklyn and Hoboken, he continues to push the boundaries of abstraction, bridging contemporary sensibilities with timeless artistic inquiries.

Petersen reflects on the influences that shaped his journey, from his Staten Island upbringing to his unexpected turn from animal science to art during his college years. He shares insights into his creative process, shaped by transformative residencies and international exhibitions, and discusses the profound impact of awards like the Barnett and Annalee Newman Foundation Grant. Join us as Petersen offers a rare glimpse into his inspirations, challenges, and hopes for the lasting impact of his art.

**How did growing up in Staten Island and studying at Pennsylvania State University influence your artistic development and**

"Gary Petersen's vibrant abstractions balance precision with spontaneity, inviting viewers into a dynamic world of color, movement, and form."

Gary Petersen's mastery of color and form infuses geometric abstraction with emotional depth, inviting viewers to experience art as connection.

**approach to painting?**

Staten Island is one of the five boroughs that make up New York City, and I grew up there in a lower-middle-class household. My parents did not have a college education, and I attended Catholic schools without any art classes. While I always had an interest in art and biology, as a first-generation college student, I felt pressure to become something rather than simply study something. When I was accepted to Pennsylvania State University, I chose to major in Animal Science, thinking I wanted to become a veterinarian. At that time, it never even crossed my mind to study art. But in my junior year, I took an art class as an elective and fell in love with it. I also began to socialize with some of the graduate art students and realized that this was what I truly wanted to pursue. I wanted to become an artist.

**You have received several prestigious residencies, including at MacDowell and the Bogliasco Foundation in Italy. How have these experiences shaped your creative process?**

The wonderful thing about artist residencies is twofold: you meet creatives outside your own field, and you're given the gift of time and space. The luxury of time at both residencies allowed me to explore new avenues in my work, free from the usual day-to-day distractions. At Bogliasco in particular, the Ligurian light and vibrant colors of the Italian cityscape inspired me to push my color palette even further.

**What was it like being awarded The Barnett and Annalee Newman Foundation Grant in 2020, and how has this recognition impacted your career?**

It was a complete surprise. After decades of work, it's wonderful to be recognized and validated for all the effort you put in. The award gave me the freedom to focus on my studio practice without financial worries, and, additionally, the Foundation purchased one of my paintings and donated it to the Jewish Museum in New York as part of the Newman Foundation collection. This prestigious collection includes many well-known artists, and it's such an honour to be a part of it.

**You've exhibited your work internationally, from New York to Munich. How does your approach differ when preparing for solo exhibitions versus group exhibitions?**

In group shows, you have limited control; the curator or art dealer installs the pieces and decides which works to include. With solo shows, however, I think more intentionally about how my work will interact with the space where it will be displayed. Since I'm always working in my studio, the gallerist often visits, and together we select the paintings for the show. We discuss which pieces work well in conversation with each other. When I know about a solo show well in advance, I also consider the sizes I want to paint and how they'll function within that specific space.

**Many prominent publications have reviewed your work over the years. How do you feel about the role of art criticism in your career and the reception of your paintings?**

I generally enjoy reading reviews of my work, as they often offer insights that give me new perspectives to consider. It's especially gratifying to read thoughtful criticism, such as John Yau's reviews of my work. He is both articulate and insightful about painting, and he can explain my work far better than I ever could.

**Your work is featured in both private and public collections, including the Dallas Museum of Art and The Jewish Museum. What do you hope viewers take away from your paintings when they see them in these different contexts?**

First, it's an honour to be included in these permanent collections. I hope my work captures the viewer's eye, drawing them in to look, connect, reflect, and perhaps experience a bit of joy. The Dallas Museum holds an earlier work compared to the piece at The Jewish Museum, but both are part of their contemporary collections, so the contexts are similar. My hope is that these works resonate with viewers about our present world and remain relevant for generations to come.

# Redefining Boundaries in Art and Space

*Anina Brisolla discusses her innovative art practice, exploring themes of privatization, environmental politics, and digitality through layered works that challenge societal structures and humanity's relationship with space and materiality.*

# ANINA BRISOLLA

## Exploring the intersections of digitality, materiality, and humanity's impact on nature and the cosmos

Editor's Desk

Anina Brisolla is a visionary artist whose work challenges the boundaries of medium, material, and meaning. Based in Berlin and the Oderbruch, her practice spans digital painting, collage, video, and installation, creating a rich tapestry of thought-provoking explorations. Brisolla's art delves into the intersections of privatization, power structures, and humanity's relationship with nature and space, offering a critical lens on the visual language of institutions and the societal shifts brought about by digitality. Her creations are as conceptually profound as they are visually striking, embodying a delicate balance between fragility and structure, the digital and the tangible, the real and the imagined.

In this exclusive interview for WOWwART Magazine, Brisolla takes us behind the scenes of her creative process, offering insights into her recent series such as "Prospect," "fabrics," and "value systems." From her intricate 3D pen sculptures to her layered explorations of space privatization and environmental politics, Brisolla's work invites us to question the systems that shape our world—and the worlds we may one day inhabit. Join us as we delve into the mind of an artist whose practice is as multifaceted as the themes she so eloquently interrogates.

**In your series 'Prospect', you explore the concept of space as a new frontier for privatization. What inspired you to address this theme through NASA and ESA imagery?**

I was looking at one image that was all over the news back then, entitled ‚New earth-like planet found'.

> "The transfer between digital and analogue media has characterized my work for a long time."

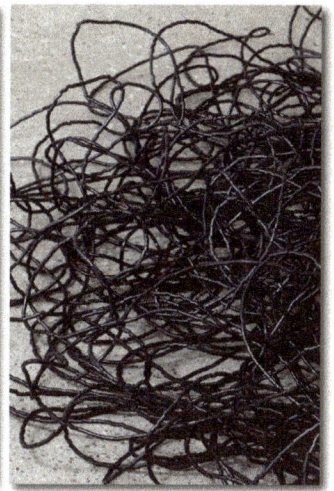

Anina Brisolla's captivating creations are a testament to her extraordinary talent and vision. Her work masterfully bridges the realms of art and technology, evoking deep emotions and sparking meaningful conversations. Each piece reflects her dedication to pushing boundaries, making her a true inspiration in the contemporary art world.

The image made me wonder what this would imply. So I printed it and started drawing directly onto the print. The image had a dark romanticism about it, almost like some sort of

> Anina Brisolla's art is a profound fusion of intellect and creativity, offering bold critiques of societal and environmental paradigms.

heavy-metal cover-artwork. That triggered me. As I continued the ‚prospect' serie, I started to work with a program similar to Google Earth, but in space. This allowed me to explore space and ‚take pictures' of sceneries stars, exoplanets,etc.

**How do you view the intersection between environmental politics and space exploration in your work, particularly with the concept of space enclosures?**

I consider fencing off an area to be an ancient cultural technique. In this we visibly separated ourselves from nature and in doing so, we have placed ourselves above nature.

What will we humans do after having destroyed this world? We fly to another planet and colonize it. And what is the first

thing we do there?

We stake out land, put up fences and take possession. This is already happening now. Not literally like in my drawings, but the race to be the first has long since begun. And even though there are regulations and acts like for example the 'Outer Space Treaty' from 1967, the economic interests are a strong engine to fuel this „New Space Economy" Space is already full of junk. Wherever men will go, a line of left behinds shows our appearance.

**Could you describe the specific process you follow to achieve the final layered look in your pieces, especially when working with large-scale images that you draw over?**

For the 'prospect' series, I worked from real models. This means that the fences and walls I drew there all have a real place in the world. My work is often preceded by intensive research and I like to use images that are anchored in the collective consciousness.

For 'prospect' for example I collected a lot of material of border fences and walls. I found it interesting to pursue questions of materiality onto another planet, so I decided for a way of drawing that is both realistic and painterly somehow and you get an idea of what the thing is made of. As the imagery often has some 'kitschy' aspect

to it, this creates an interesting tension.

**Shifting between different media, from video to installation, seems to be a key aspect of your work. What influences your decision to choose one medium over another for specific projects?**

A new project usually arises from direct involvement with a specific topic, reading or watching a documentary for example. I have always been interested in how digitalization affects society. And at the same time, the transfer between digital and analogue media is an idea that has characterized my work for a long time. For me, it therefore seems just logical to include the choice of working material in the conceptual process with every new project.

Sometimes I work with a kind of 'reverse engineering' and that also determines the final result.

Some of my work of recent years deals with the process of 3D printing in this analytical way. I replaced the mechanics of the print head, which is calculated and controlled by the computer, with the movement of my hand along predetermined lines of movement.

**Could you explain the significance of the 40,000-bead installation '8 Milliarden' in your SMAC exhibition and how it complements the other works?**

'8 Milliarden' - 8 billion

- corresponds to the current population of the world. In my exhibition called 'space mining' at SMAC I created work along three timelines: past – present – future.

'8 Milliarden' is thus to be seen as the present. I wanted to see the world's population manifested and at the same time know for myself how big this pile would be. There is an addition to the title: M 1:200.000. This is the scale in which the work is carried out. So one pearl corresponds to the population of a middle sized city such as Kassel here in Germany or i.e. Norwich in the UK.

'space mining' denotes the concept of mining raw materials in space. Optimistic scientists predict that in twenty years' time, it will likely be possible to apply those techniques. Globalization has mapped the world anew and revealed the finitude of raw materials. The quest for resources has always inspired the human spirit - and attempts to pursue them have had a lasting impact on human history. This is where I started my artistic reflection on the topic, questioning the motives of the actors involved. I conceived this model of the present in order to use it as a starting point for these considerations.

Janet Hennessey Dilenschneider brings her unique perspective to life, creating serene landscapes that encourage a deeper connection with the environment.

*Painting Hope and Harmony*

# JANET HENNESSEY DILENSCHNEIDER

## How Nature and Expressionism Shape Her Visionary Art

as told to Hazel Ivy

*"Janet Hennessey Dilenschneider, an expressionist painter, draws inspiration from nature to create serene landscapes. Her work emphasizes hope and beauty, encouraging viewers to connect with art and environmental issues."*

In the world of contemporary art, few artists capture the ethereal beauty and profound serenity of nature quite like Janet Hennessey Dilenschneider. From her early beginnings, when a chance encounter with the legendary Roy Lichtenstein set her on a path of artistic discovery, to her current status as a celebrated expressionist painter, Dilenschneider's journey is as inspiring as her work. Her paintings, characterized by rich palettes, loose brush strokes, and luminous misty vistas, invite viewers to experience the world through her eyes—where light and color dance in harmonious symphony.

We're proud to feature Janet Hennessey Dilenschneider on our cover, celebrating her unique ability to convey hope and tranquility through her art. Her latest exhibition, "Come To The Light," is a testament to her commitment to providing peace and solace in a troubled world. By drawing inspiration from the natural beauty of her Connecticut surroundings and the broader global landscape, Dilenschneider's work resonates with a universal message of renewal and inspiration.

In this exclusive interview, we delve into the creative process behind her evocative landscapes, her influences from impressionism and expressionism, and her dedication to using art as a medium for social commentary. As she continues to evolve and explore new themes, Janet Hennessey Dilenschneider remains a beacon of artistic innovation and a testament to the transformative power of art. Join us as we explore the mind and heart of an artist who invites us all to fall in love with nature—and ourselves—all over again. Your exhibition Come To The Light emphasizes the serenity and beauty of nature.

**Can you share more about your creative process and how your surroundings in Connecticut influence your work?**

My surroundings PLUS what is happening in the world GREATLY affects my paintings. With "Come To The Light" my objective is to give PEACE and SOLACE to a troubled world… thus, to give INSPIRATION and HOPE.

**Continued** *on page 66*  ➜

Continued *on page 66*

**Continued** *from page 65*

SPRING TREES, 24 X 30

*A vibrant celebration of renewal, this painting captures the essence of spring with its lively colors and dynamic composition, inviting viewers to experience the rejuvenating energy of nature's awakening.*

When, one very early morning, I passed a second-floor window and saw the beautiful sunrise, I was impressed beyond belief and motivated to paint that sunrise. I then thought, this is the THEME of the show. I followed with mostly paintings which had lovely reflections of sun on water or giving highlights to some object. Light and sun are inspiring to many people, even spiritual to some.

**You had a memorable encounter with Roy Lichtenstein early in your career. How did that experience shape your journey as an artist, and are there any other pivotal moments that have influenced your artistic path?**

Yes, at about 16, I entered a painting in a formal juried show, for the first time. Initially, I was rejected and very disappointed. A man offered to help me by putting the required hanging wires on the back. I subsequently learned it was Roy Lichtenstein and the curator of the show. Later a friend called and said I had won first place in Water Color. How motivating!

Other moments were when a teacher in an art class pulled me aside and suggested I major in art. It seemed so obvious then.

One of the most professionally motivating moments was when an important gallery owner in Paris that we had just

had dinner with looked at my work on a CD and said, "Well, I guess we are just going to have to give you a show" … my first SOLO show and in Paris! That was 2013 and I have had 14 solo shows since them, 7 as a result of my Paris gallery exhibition.

**The title of your exhibition, "Come To The Light," suggests a sense of hope and tranquility. What message or emotions do you hope to convey to viewers through this collection of paintings?**

I want whomever needs a little "hope" or reinforcement to get the spiritual feeling from the paintings and allow themselves to feel a sense of renewal. Art

*Surrounded by her vibrant landscapes, Janet Hennessey Dilenschneider finds inspiration in the natural world to create art that speaks to the soul.*

**Continued** *on page 67*

ROAD THROUGH PROVENCE, 24 X 36

*This captivating piece transports viewers to the sun-drenched landscapes of Provence, where winding roads lead through fields of color and light, capturing the serene beauty and timeless charm of the region.*

GLORIOUS SUNSET, OIL ON CANVAS, 24 X 30

*This stunning painting captures the breathtaking beauty of a sunset, with vibrant hues and masterful brushwork that evoke the warmth and tranquility of the day's end.*

can be healing and motivational if we allow it to be.

As an artist, I have a personal obligation to give something to my viewer. My objective is to have them participate in the painting and get something out of it.

**You are known for your expressionist style with influences from impressionism. Can you discuss how these styles have impacted your work and how you have developed your unique artistic voice over the years?**

As an Expressionist painter, I want you to FEEL what I feel and like about that tree. How do I attempt to do this? I use very free brushstrokes, if the strokes are angled and deftly put down, they are to me the PASSION in the painting. This PASSION is shown through the GESTURE lines and colors laid down next to each other.

The color is the JOY, not just one color but the combination of colors. One color can "modify" how you see the other – they add excitement. They "sing" together as I like to say. This is called "simultaneous contrast," and it is often used today. It is, however, revered and borrowed from the Impressionists, that and their freedom of stroke are the two greatest concepts they gave us. They freed up the way for Abstract Expressionists and

today's contemporary artists.

**With several exhibitions planned for later this year, can you give us a glimpse into what you are working on next and any new themes or ideas you are excited to explore in your upcoming projects?**

I am currently working on new techniques and subject matter. An artist needs to constantly evolve and challenge their own artistry and bring it to new heights. I am in love with the shapes of clouds and "misting out" landscape scenes.

**You mentioned that your passion for the arts was "inherited" from your mother and sister. How did their influence shape your artistic style and career, and are there specific lessons or techniques you learned from them that you still use today?**

I was surrounded with art as a youngster. My mother's paintings were very realistic. If I were her art teacher, I would have suggested she "free up" her brushstroke, however, her colors were beautiful. I still remember sitting at the breakfast table as a young girl with my sister and she told us, "Always put your lightest lights next to your darkest darks." I do use this technique today, and I also use it as a philosophy of life.

**You've expressed a desire for**

*Janet Hennessey Dilenschneider brings her unique perspective to life, creating serene landscapes that encourage a deeper connection with the environment.*

**Continued** *on page 68*

**Continued** *from page 67*

artists to comment on societal issues, particularly ecology and global warming. How do you balance conveying a message about these critical issues while also creating art that provides a sense of peace and beauty?

Good question. I do believe artists have the right, even the obligation, to make reference to social change.

I try to get the viewer to "Participate" in the painting and see the point of view I have about the issue. In my first solo shows, I wanted to have the viewer "fall in love with nature all over again" as I like to say. My goal was to develop an awareness of the ecology.

I showed beautiful trees, greenery and leaves which everyone could appreciate. Now, recently I have tried to get the viewer to feel that sense of calm and renewal which the "Come To The Light" Exhibition has shown.

I do believe a painting can affect a person. The way I reflect ecology, global warming, and conflict in the world that causes unrest is to treat the subjects with calming and beautiful images. Beauty in the art is what does the work.

Can you elaborate on your creative process, particularly how you let your "creative brain" take over when interpreting colors and designs? How do experiences, like your drive through Provence, influence your work?

The "Creative Process" is many things: very easy, complicated and interpretive. I always look at all visual stimuli, specially if I am looking for something to "spark" a painting. I try to never copy but as many famous artists have said, "let the paint take you and tell you where to go." This is where your "creative brain" should take over. You have been sending artistic messages and images to your "artistic brain" for a long time. Now you work on your painting and look for the "new-

> *Janet H. Dilenschneider's masterful use of color and light creates a breathtaking vista that stretches beyond the canvas, symbolizing infinite possibilities.*

**SUNRISE, COME TO THE LIGHT, 36 X 48**

*Janet's evocative painting invites viewers to embrace the dawn's first light, with its radiant colors and dynamic composition symbolizing hope and new beginnings.*

**Continued** *on page 69*

**Continued** *from page 68*

GREEN RUSHES İNTO YELLOW GRASSES, 30 X 30

*Janet's vibrant painting beautifully captures the interplay of nature's colors, where lilac reflections blend into golden grasses, evoking a sense of calm and excitement to the color contrast.*

ness" you want to create.

My ride through Provence was a perfect example. There were many beautiful treelined allées and I had the driver stop at least 8 times to photograph them. I was enchanted with the scenes, the colors, shadows, and winding roads. Five paintings were the result. None are exactly alike in color or style. This was one of my "Creative Brain" escapades.

**You've had the opportunity to do solo exhibitions in various locations. How does the freedom to paint what you feel and see impact your work, and are there any particular themes or subjects you are eager to explore in future exhibitions?**

What one "feels" about what one sees is what it is all about. If you don't have a feeling about the scene, go to the next scene. Right now, I am into

CLOUDS and how to paint them with a "misty" look. They are magical. I am also in love with ATMOSPHERE and how it is shimmery and misty with one color blending into another. That is where I am going now with my brush. There is a lot of violence in the world today. I won't paint THAT! I want people to be uplifted and enlightened, I paint the "Light" not the "Dark."

**You advise young painters to "beat their own drum" and "observe, observe, observe." Can you share more about how emerging artists can find their unique voice and the importance of being attuned to the world around them in their creative journey?**

I always advise young artists to LOOK at everything they can: art books of favorite artists, art magazines, galleries, museums. Spend some time learning about

what others have done. Spend some good time on this and then do your personal research. Look at the different shapes of leaves in a garden, or of clouds floating by, or colors next to each other in a flower garden. Then let your "Creative Brain" take over. Always remember GESTURE which is Design of the piece and COLOR which is the biggest attraction …. and the JOY.

The Chinese artists say, "Draw it 9 times; paint it once." Try that too
Source: Mosaic Digest

# Empowering Young Readers Through Fiction and Digital Awareness

# CRAIG FORD

# Blends Cybersecurity with Storytelling

BY ELEANOR WILSON | LONDON

Craig Ford is a force to be reckoned with—equal parts cyber expert, educator, and imaginative storyteller. With a background deeply rooted in cybersecurity, Ford has taken an extraordinary leap from technical writing into the dynamic world of young adult fiction and children's literature, and the results are nothing short of inspiring. His award-winning books Foresight and The Shadow World don't just entertain—they educate, empower, and ignite curiosity in readers of all ages, particularly young women and children who are so often left

---

*Craig Ford blends his cybersecurity expertise with creative storytelling to empower young readers, break stereotypes, and promote digital awareness through acclaimed books like Foresight and The Shadow World.*

---

out of conversations about technology.

At Mosaic Digest Magazine, we are proud to spotlight authors who aren't afraid to challenge stereotypes, break barriers, and use their craft to create meaningful change. Through his compelling characters and real-world experience, Ford dismantles outdated notions about hacking and gender roles in tech, replacing them with empowering narratives that show cyber is not just a boy's club—and never was.

In this insightful interview, Craig Ford shares the motivations behind his work, the powerful message behind his characters, and his ongoing mission to build a more cyber-aware world. His passion for technology and inclusivity shines through every word, and we're honoured to share his voice with our readers.

**Your background in cybersecurity is extensive. What inspired you to transition from technical writing to crafting young adult fiction like Foresight?**

Foresight was born out of a desire to help encourage more young women an interest in Cyber Security. I had been writing a regular column for the Women in Security Magazine and I wanted to do more. What could I do as a man in the industry, as a writer. Well, I chose to create Sam (Samantha) a teenage hacker and show my readers that cyber is cool, its not just a boys club and give them a character that is based on real world experience in this space so they can go – Wow maybe I could be her.

It also gives men in the industry a new perspective, seeing an amazing female character, change minds both boys and Girls for the better.

Oh and it was also really fun to dive down the rabbit hole for my readers to get a picture of the hacker world.

**In Foresight, you introduce Samantha, a teenage hacker navigating complex digital challenges. How did you develop her character, and what message do you hope she conveys to readers?**

I wanted to create a character to inspire young women, to show them that cyber is a cool career choice. Outside of that I wanted to show readers what the hacker world is like, yes with a little bit of a Hollywood flare (you can't have a reader engaged if a hack takes 6 months to achieve). I think its important to have that real world character, someone that could be you, it could be the girl next door and have it break the hacker in the hoodie stereotype that has long plagued the industry.

I am more likely to wear a suit then a hoodie and that is true for most hackers in this space. So basically I wanted to break the mould of two stereotypes – Hacker hoodies and that this is a boys club. Its neither of those things in reality.

**You've co-authored The Shadow World, a children's book on cyber safety. What motivated you to create educational content for younger audiences, and how has the reception been?**

The Shadow World is an amazing book that I am very proud to have coauthored. Teaching kids as young as 5-6 how to safely navigate the online world is super important, we need to set real world behaviours at a really young age before the bad behaviours that many adults have are set in. It is much harder to break the lifetime of bad habbits then it is to teach that right way, right from the start.

The response and feedback has been massively positive. It reached best seller status withing weeks of being released and with recent awards it doesn't appear to be slowing down.

**Both Foresight and The Shadow World have received accolades, including recognition from the Independent Press Award. How have these honors impacted your mission to promote cyber education?**

These awards are amazing at helping to continue to drive my mission to educate the world on cyber safety. It will help the new cyber education platform we have just launched with a mobile app to really give everyday people the essential cyber awareness right across mums and dads, seniors, kids and small businesses.

This passion to bridge the gap will likely drive me to both grow this platform and create many more books in the future. Its too important not to drive change where I can. These awards and others will definitely help do that.

**As a male author writing a strong female protagonist in a male-dominated field, how do you approach authenticity and representation in your storytelling?**

I am a little lucky as I have five sisters, so I have a little insight but honestly I have an amazing editor Steph who ensured I walked the line correctly as I wanted to ensure it was authentic and really hit the mark with my target audience.

Its always hard to try to ensure you do it justice though but I feel like I have done reasonably well with Foresight and my character Sam.

**With the rapid evolution of technology, what future topics or themes do you plan to explore in your upcoming works to continue educating and engaging your readers?**

100% it is moving at lightning speed, its hard to keep pace sometimes but I would like to explore the autonomous vehicles more, I think there is a lot that is going to happen in this area especially as AI and quantum computing really explodes. It is a very interesting world we are living in over the next decade and I think I am going to continue to find inspertaion of both my novels and educational books from these three spaces.

The crazy thing to consider is what technologies will be coming that we cant even contemplate yet, robotics/AI and so much more is happening. What is next.

**Craig Ford:** *Cybersecurity Expert And Award-Winning Author On A Mission To Educate And Inspire Through Stories*

" *I wanted to show readers that cyber is cool; it's not just a boys' club.*"

# Craig Ford

# Exploring the Journey

as told to J. Evans

## Master Storyteller Across Mediums

Thomas White's journey from the theater to the literary world is a testament to the power of storytelling in all its forms. Beginning his career as an actor, White quickly transitioned to directing, earning accolades such as Drama-Logue and Critics awards. His role as Artistic Director for a Los Angeles theater set the stage for his future endeavors, including the world tour of "*The Teenage Mutant Ninja Turtles: Coming Out Of Their Shells,*" which captivated nearly a million children worldwide. With a career spanning over two decades as President and Creative Director of Maiden Lane Entertainment, White has orchestrated large-scale corporate events for giants like Harley Davidson and Microsoft. Now, as an acclaimed author, he continues to weave compelling narratives, with his latest novel, "The Edison Enigma," adding to his growing literary repertoire.

White's diverse background in theater and event production has profoundly influenced his approach to writing. "*As a director, you tell stories using actors, sets, props, and lighting. As an author, you use your words,*" he explains. This seamless transition from stage to page underscores his belief that the core objective remains the same: to engage the audience emotionally. Whether through a theatrical production or a novel, White's goal is to captivate and entertain, ensuring that the audience remains invested from beginning to end.

*The Edison Enigma*, White's third novel, delves into the intriguing concept of time travel and the consequences of altering history. The inspiration for this theme came from a corporate event for Saturn in 1997, where the electric car, the EV-1, was unveiled. Years later, an article titled "The Death Of The Electric Car" sparked White's curiosity about the historical trajectory of electric vehicles. His research revealed a series of coincidences at the turn of the 20th century, leading him to imagine a scenario where the world chose electric cars over internal combustion engines. This imaginative leap forms the crux of *The Edison Enigma*, blending science fiction with historical speculation to create a thought-provoking narrative.

In *The Siren's Scream,* White explores the eerie Thornton Mansion and its mysterious tide pool, a setting that exudes suspense and dread. Initially inspired by mermaid myths, White sought to breathe new life into the well-worn trope. The idea of mermaids dealing with familial conflicts and lineage sparked a storyline that evolved into a gripping tale of mystery and intrigue. By reimagining the mermaid mythos, White crafted a novel that stands out in the genre, offering readers a fresh perspective on an ancient legend.

*Justice Rules*, White's debut novel, centers on FBI Special Agent Brian Wylie and a vigilante coalition. The plot was inspired by the aftermath of the OJ Simpson trial, particularly the emotional devastation of Ron Goldman's father, Fred. This poignant moment led White to ponder the lengths one might go to seek justice outside the legal system. The resulting narrative explores themes of justice and morality, challenging readers to consider the complexities of revenge and retribution.

Recognition as a finalist in the Pacific Northwest Writers Association 2010 Literary contest for "Justice Rules" was a significant milestone in White's writing career. Although he did not immediately follow up with another novel, the nomination affirmed his talent and potential as a writer. Reflecting on the experience, White acknowledges the honour but also the overwhelming nature of his accomplishment, which led to a decade-long hiatus before his next literary endeavor.

Balancing the creative demands of writing novels with the logistical challenges of producing events is no small feat, yet White finds parallels between the two processes. "*I always describe my career as being someone in production,*" he says. Whether producing plays, corporate events, or novels, the skill set remains consistent: envisioning a project and bringing it to life. The blank page, much like an empty stage, represents both a challenge and an opportunity for creativity to flourish.

Thomas White's multifaceted career exemplifies the versatility and resilience of a true storyteller. From the theater to the corporate world and now to the realm of literature, his ability to engage and entertain remains unwavering. As he continues to craft new narratives, readers can look forward to more captivating tales from this accomplished author.

Thomas White's storytelling prowess and creative versatility make him a standout author, seamlessly blending history, imagination, and emotion.

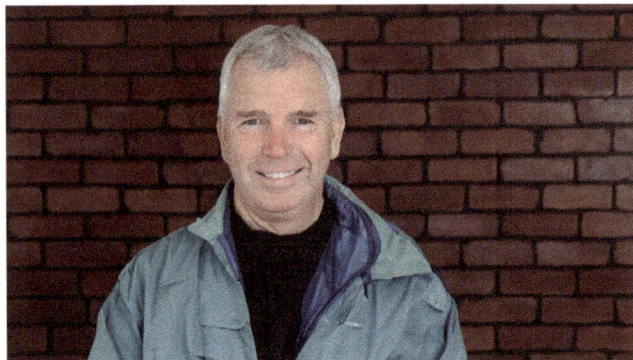

> " *I always describe my career as being someone in production. I produce plays, musicals, sales events, corporate meetings, product reveals, novels, etc. The skill set is pretty much the same, you create a vision in your head, then utilize your skill set to make it come to life. Writer's always talk about the blank piece of paper and how there is nothing scarier. That is 100% true.*

## Thomas White

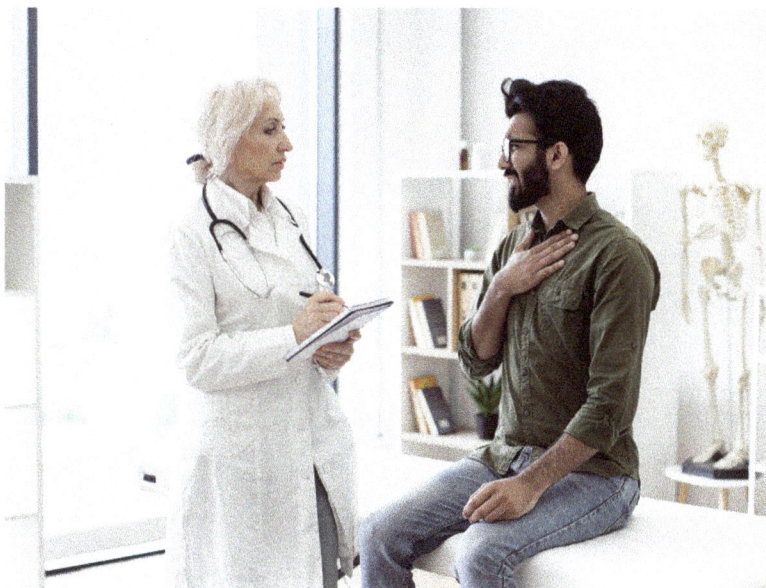

# Shortness of Breath Not Going Away?
## Ask Your Doctor for a Blood Test

*Pulmonary alveolar proteinosis (PAP) is a rare lung disease often misdiagnosed due to symptom similarities with other conditions. The American Lung Association's campaign aims to improve aPAP awareness and diagnosis.*

Pulmonary alveolar proteinosis (PAP) is an ultra-rare lung disease with approximately 3,600 diagnosed cases in the United States. Unfortunately, some people are potentially living with the disease without knowing it, as it is often misdiagnosed.

That is why the American Lung Association, with support from Savara Inc., is launching a new educational campaign to help healthcare providers and patients better recognize the signs and symptoms of autoimmune pulmonary alveolar proteinosis, (aPAP), the most common form of the disease. As part of the campaign, they are sharing these fast facts:

What is aPAP? This disease is characterized by the abnormal buildup of surfactant in the air sacs of the lungs, which can make breathing difficult. The buildup is due to an inability to clear the surfactant. Occurring in both males and females, aPAP is often diagnosed between the ages of 30 and 60.

What are its symptoms? Some people who are living with aPAP may not show symptoms initially, while others may have progressive shortness of breath. Additional symptoms include chronic cough, fatigue, unintentional weight loss and chest pain.

Why is aPAP commonly misdiagnosed? Since aPAP is so rare, and because symptoms are similar to other more common lung diseases, it is often misdiagnosed. Common misdiagnoses include both acute and chronic lung diseases such as pneumonia and asthma.

How is aPAP diagnosed? If you are diagnosed with another lung disease and the treatment is not effective, your doctor may recommend a chest CT scan. If you have an abnormal chest scan with unresolved lung symptoms, you should also talk to your healthcare provider about getting a free, simple blood test called aPAP ClearPath, which measures the level of the GM-CSF antibodies in your blood to determine if you have the disease.

How is aPAP treated? Currently, there is no cure for aPAP and no FDA-approved therapies; however, symptoms can be managed. The most common treatment is whole lung lavage, (WLL) also called "lung washing." WLL washes out the built-up surfactant from the lungs, allowing you to breathe more easily. This treatment often needs to be repeated, as it doesn't address the underlying cause of the disease.

Managing aPAP well means seeing a specialist who is familiar with this rare lung disease and going to all of your regularly scheduled healthcare appointments.

To learn more, visit Lung. org/PAP.

Without treatment, this progressive disease can increase the risk of infection and lead to respiratory failure that may become life threatening. Don't wait. Talk to your doctor if your respiratory symptoms are not being managed with current treatments.

**CEO VISION** INSIDER

ceovision.co.uk
Jan-Feb · 2026
GLOBAL EDITION

## Perry Offer's Vision for Modern Business

Why Leaders Must Rethink Complexity to Thrive in a Competitive World

## Ethics Meets Innovation: The Global Rise of Islamic Finance · projected growth to $9.7 trillion by 2029

Exclusive Interviews with Game-Changers from Tech, Finance, Retail, and More

Available in
**PRINT**

It can be found in over 190 countries, from the Americas to Australia and Europe to Africa. It is accessible through thousands of retailers and platforms, including Amazon, Barnes & Noble, Walmart, and Waterstones.

**ELECTRONIC**

It is available in an electronic flip book format and is interactive. You can access it from various electronic devices, including PCs, smartphones, and tablets.

**ONLINE**

All the interviews we conduct are accessible online at no cost.

contact us today for an interview opportunity at
editor@ceovision.co.uk

CEO VISION INSIDER

# Key Partnerships and Future Initiatives
## Expanding the Boundaries of Art and Media

*Being featured in CEO VISION INSIDER means gaining visibility not just in print edition, but across the entire media spectrum in the US, UK, Europe and beyond*

## Key Media Partnerships:

- Associated Press (reaching 50%+ of global population)
- Benzinga (5M monthly visitors)
- Nexstar (68% U.S. TV household penetration)
- Major search engines: Google News, Google, Yahoo, Bing, Ask
- EIN Press Wire coverage
- NewYox Media magazines coverage (Mosaic Digest, Reader's House, CEO Vision Inside , Novelist Post, Beauty Prime...)

## Broadcast & Digital Coverage:

- Major U.S. network affiliates
- 150+ million monthly radio website users
- 500+ UK media outlets
- Minimum 5 to 20 media placements per country (Albania to Zambia)
- Enhanced SEO positioning with quality backlinks from each media
- Optimized presence on e-commerce platforms)

## Distribution Highlights:

- Available through major retailers including Amazon, Barnes & Noble, Walmart, Blackwells and Waterstones
- Available through local retailers Alaska to Wisconsin in the United States.
- Available in print LIFETIME
- Featured across 3000+ media platforms in the US, UK, Europe and beyond

contact us today for an interview opportunity at
editor@ceovision.co.uk